# DEDICATION

For Bob Battle and Elizabeth Ogilvie Battle.
There's no place like home in Tennessee,
but St. Louis comes pretty close.

SECOND
EDITION

# What's with St. Louis?

## Valerie Battle Kienzle

REEDY PRESS

# CONTENTS

**PREFACE, 1**

**SECTION 1—FOOD, 2**

**What's with the pretzel guys on every corner?**

Life with a twist, 2

**Who put white Velveeta on my pizza?**

Provel—a St. Louis original, 4

**"I'd like a Greek salad, a burek, and a cerveza, please."**

St. Louis, home of specialty foods from around the world, 6

**Brain on rye? With onions?**

The original brain food, 8

**Ravioli can be fried? Who knew?**

Toasted ravioli—only in St. Louis, 10

**Pork steaks sound fancy, butt . . .**

The Lou's love of pork steaks, 12

**Another wedding, another plate of mostaccioli**

A St. Louis wedding reception tradition, 14

**The slinger**

St. Louis's cure for late-night cravings, 16

**Donut obsessed, perhaps?**

St. Louisans love that fried dough. 18

**How can cake be gooey?**

Gooey butter cake—a St. Louis specialty, 20

**Why are fish fries so popular in St. Louis?**

Meatless Friday cheats, 22

**SECTION 2—WEATHER, 24**

**Why do I feel like I'm in an outdoor sauna?**

The Lou's high humidity, 24

SECOND EDITION

# What's with St. Louis?

REEDY PRESS

Library of Congress Control Number: 2018945697

ISBN: 9781681061849

Design by Jill Halpin

Printed in the United States of America
19 20 21 22  5 4 3 2

**Is an earthquake really possible?**

New Madrid, the San Andreas of the Midwest, 26

**Auntie Em, why is everyone running to the basement?**

St. Louis—a severe weather magnet, 28

**SECTION 3—WATER, 30**

**This so-called river is everywhere, but where's the water?**

The River des Peres, St. Louis's man-made waterway, 30

**The Mississippi River looks pretty brown and determined—like those big birds over there.**

Bald eagles and other migratory birds spend their winters in St. Louis. 32

**Waterworks standpipes**

Early water towers combined form and function. 34

**The St. Louis District of the U.S. Army Corps of Engineers—Important and Understated**

They keep things going. 36

**SECTION 4—DRINK UP, 38**

**More breweries than you can shake a stein at**

St. Louisans love their beer. 38

**The ghosts of soft drinks past**

St. Louis, an incubator for soft drink development, 40

**Anyone from here sleeping with the fishes?**

St. Louis's organized crime connection, 42

**SECTION 5—WHAT'S IN A WORD? 44**

**Hoosier? But I'm not from Indiana.**

The peculiar vocabulary of St. Louisans, 44

**Hey, yous guys!**

Uniquely St. Louis pronunciations, 46

**The Fourth City? What were the first three?**

St. Louis, one of America's top cities, 48

## SECTION 6—STREET TALK, 50

**How did I pass through eight cities in three miles driving down one road?**

St. Louis and the abundance of small municipalities, 50

**The rolling stop—a St. Louis tradition**

How St. Louisans view stop signs, 52

**Can you still get your kicks on Route 66?**

The Mother Road is still alive in St. Louis. 54

**Cherokee Street (more than a people, more than a tribe)**

A popular St. Louis street and neighborhood, 56

**Why are St. Louis's downtown streets named for trees?**

An arborist's delight, 58

**Riding the rails**

Railroading in St. Louis, 60

**I'm on Lindbergh Blvd., wait North Kirkwood Road, wait Lindbergh? And why isn't one Watson enough?**

St. Louis streets and unexpected name changes, 62

**Why are there so many one-way streets in St. Louis?**

But I was only going one way. 64

**What's in a name?**

Every street name tells a story. 66

**Urban blight becomes eclectic delight.**

Rebirth of the University City Loop, 68

**Do you believe in ghosts?**

Ghost signs of St. Louis, 70

**Why are there pieces of metal track in South St. Louis that lead nowhere?**

The tracks to nowhere, 72

## SECTION 7—TREASURES, 74

**Soulard Farmers Market**

Something for everyone, 74

**How did so many museums end up so close to each other?**

St. Louis's abundance of free museums, 76

**City Museum**

One person's trash is another's treasure. 78

**This zoo is a pretty big deal, isn't it?**

St. Louis's world-class zoo, 80

**Does that building really mean no harm to our planet?**

James S. McDonnell Planetarium at the Saint Louis
Science Center, 82

**What's that building that looks like a cross between
a bird's nest and a jungle gym?**

The Climatron, a unique St. Louis structural gem, 102

**Singing the blues**

The National Blues Museum calls St. Louis home. 104

**A big stainless steel parabola**

The Gateway Arch, 106

**A witness to history**

The Old Courthouse, 108

**What's the story behind the Eads Bridge?**

A bridge ahead of its time, 110

**SECTION 8—HISTORIC INFLUENCES, 112**

**St. Louis's French connection continues today.**

Subtle nods to the Founding Fathers' heritage, 112

**What role did St. Louis play in the civil rights movement?**

Equality for all, 114

**The Civil War**

Important considerations, 116

**SECTION 9—UNIQUELY ST. LOUIS, 118**

**"Where'd you go to high school?" and other St. Louis
questions**

How St. Louisans categorize each other, 118

**I see it's a garage sale, but where's the garage?**

The unspoken rules of St. Louis garage sales, 120

**Why was St. Louis called the Mound City? Do they like candy bars that much?**

Ancient civilizations dug St. Louis. 122

**Why is that guy Ted Drewes so popular? Is he giving away bags of money?**

Frozen custard's popularity in the Lou, 124

**What sayeth the Veiled Prophet? And doeth we care?**

St. Louis and its storied traditions, 126

**Here's to your health!**

St. Louis hospitals offer hope and healing. 128

**Was St. Louis really first in shoes?**

Walk a mile (or more) in our shoes. 130

**Who is this Sweetmeat character and should I avoid him?**

Never too old to rock and roll, 132

**What's the only Vatican-verified miracle to have occurred in the Midwest?**

It's a miracle! 134

**SECTION 10—URBAN OASES, 136**

**Public parks both large and small**

St. Louis's abundance of green spaces, 136

**Grant's Farm**

St. Louis's other animal park, 138

**I see dead people. With cool headstones.**

Bellefontaine and Calvary Cemeteries—where the in-crowd spends eternity, 140

**Why does the Missouri Botanical Garden contain a Japanese garden?**

A pocket of serene beauty, 142

**SECTION 11—SPORTS, 144**

**Is Cardinals Nation a religious group?**

Almost. St. Louis has baseball fever. 144

**The St. Louis Blues are more than just a hockey team.**

St. Louis and its Blue Note fans, 146

**Gone but not forgotten**

St. Louis's lost sports franchises, 148

**St. Louis Arena**

The Old Barn, 150

**Why are St. Louisans so obsessed with soccer?**

Who's got the ball? 152

**What is bocce?**

A timeless game for all ages, 154

**SECTION 12—WHERE WE LIVE, 156**

**Livin' just enough for the city . . . which is different from living in the county; or City Mouse, County Mouse.**

St. Louis City and St. Louis County, a unique municipal arrangement, 156

**Brick, brick everywhere; or St. Louis 3, Big Bad Wolf 0.**

The abundance of brick homes and buildings in St. Louis, 158

**Why did the Italians seek high ground?**

Topography contributed to this St. Louis neighborhood's nickname. 160

**What's up with all the four-family flats?**

St. Louis and its building trends, 162

**You call these skyscrapers?**

St. Louis—a leader in architectural style, 164

**Wait . . . you had to leave home to take a bath?**

St. Louis's municipal bathhouses, 166

**Why does St. Louis have a large Bosnian population?**

Welcome to St. Louis, Missouri, USA, 168

**SECTION 13—UP IN THE AIR, 170**

**The spirit of flight**

St. Louis's aeronautical connection, 170

**My beautiful balloon**

St. Louis's love of hot-air balloons, 172

**SECTION 14—THE FAIR, 174**

**This city is fairly infatuated with 1904.**

When the world came to St. Louis, 174

**St. Louis really hosted an Olympics?**

St. Louis's Olympic connection, 176

**SECTION 15—WORSHIP, PLAY, WEAR, 178**

**Turn right at the Catholic church. No, not that one,
the other one.**

The St. Louis Catholic connection, 178

**This town looks sleepy for a Saturday night.**

Some St. Louis neighborhoods come to life after dark. 180

**Over one hundred years old, but still called new?**

Cathedral Basilica of Saint Louis—the New Cathedral, 182

**What is Holy Corners?**

Houses of worship + beautiful architecture = timeless
beauty, 184

**St. Louis is a party city? Welcome to Party Town!**

St. Louisans love a good civic party or parade or reason
to celebrate. 186

**Where the wares were wearable.**

St. Louis's connection to the shoe and clothing industries, 188

**Bibliography, 190**
**Photo Credits, 205**
**Index, 206**

# PREFACE

STL. The Gateway City. St. Louie. Arch City. The Lou. River City. Rome of the West. Mound City. All are nicknames (or were nicknames) for St. Louis, Missouri. Whether you're new to the area or a lifelong resident whose ancestors settled here generations ago, St. Louis has much to offer.

What's with this Gateway to the West city located miles from the east and west coasts? Look up. Look down. Look around. No really, look around St. Louis. Exciting things are happening here. Like a colorful patchwork quilt, St. Louis is composed of a variety of people, influences, neighborhoods, activities, architectural treasures, and foods that contribute to its overall unique character and flavor. From big-city style to urban hip culture to old-fashioned small-town charm, the St. Louis area has it all.

Want a bird's-eye view of St. Louis? Take a trip to City Museum's rooftop playground. Or climb the steps to the very top row of Busch Stadium. Hop aboard one of the Gateway Arch's tram capsules, motor your way to the top, and take a peek out the observation windows. Want to see, taste, and feel the heart and soul of this two-hundred-plus-year-old River City? Visit some of its many ethnically diverse neighborhoods. *This* is St. Louis.

St. Louisans value cultural and educational institutions, embrace diversity, and are die-hard fans of their sports teams. Want to know more about St. Louis and those who call it home? Turn the page.

Valerie Battle Kienzle

# What's with the pretzel guys on every corner?

## Life with a twist

Maybe you've seen them. They hawk paper-wrapped pretzel sticks before sporting events and during rush-hour traffic. The packaging is simple, but one taste will convince you that these pretzels are amazing.

St. Louis is one of only three major U.S. cities where vendors sell pretzels on street corners. Gus' Pretzels, a fourth-generation family business and a St. Louis favorite, has supplied pretzels to street vendors for generations. "Street vendors in St. Louis are a solid tradition that hasn't changed for years," says Gus Koebbe III. "Beer and pretzels go hand in hand, and beer and pretzels have been a part of St. Louis for a long time."

## "Beer and pretzels go hand in hand."

 FOOD

Pretzels were popular in Europe for centuries. The arrival of street-vendor pretzels coincided with the influx of German immigrants to St. Louis in the early twentieth century. The pretzels sold on the street weren't hard and crunchy.

They were tasty, soft, chewy sticks—and St. Louisans loved them. Since 1920, Gus' has combined the same basic ingredients and no preservatives. "We keep it simple and try to put out the best product possible each day. We make twelve hundred three-ounce pretzel sticks a day and usually sell out."

# Who put white Velveeta on my pizza?

**Provel—a St. Louis original**

## "I'll have Provel on that." Or not.

Unless you're placing a food order in the St. Louis area, this request may be met with a blank stare.

Or a follow-up question like, *"You mean provolone?"*

🥄🍴🔪 **FOOD**

Provel isn't the same as provolone cheese. Provel is a uniquely St. Louis food product obtained by combining three cheeses—processed cheddar, Swiss, and provolone. This combo results in a product that's creamy and less stringy when heated.

Put it on pizza, melt it on a sandwich or mound it on a salad. However it's served, Provel is a favorite St. Louis taste sensation. The origins of Provel cheese are somewhat a mystery, with several St. Louis families claiming their ancestors created and introduced it in the late 1940s. U.S. Patent and Trademark Office records reveal the product was trademarked in 1950 and that the name Provel has no meaning—it's just a jumble of letters.

Provel was popularized locally in the mid-1960s with the introduction of another St. Louis original—Imo's pizza. With its incredibly thin crust, creamy melted Provel, and other toppings, Imo's is crave-worthy. Plus Provel can be ordered and shipped from Imo's.

## Fact BOX

Provel is a versatile food product. It has a low melting point, and at room temperature, has a gooey, almost buttery texture. Provel can be purchased in loaf or rope form. Unlike some cheese products, it can be frozen for up to two months without damaging the quality or taste, unless it remains frozen so long it gets crystals and freezer burn. At that point, don't have great expectations.

# I'd like a Greek salad, a burek, and a cerveza, please.

## St. Louis, home of specialty foods from around the world

One of the great things about an ethnically diverse population is the food. So many recipes for combining ingredients to produce unique, delicious results.

Think of St. Louis as a melting pot of people, customs, and foods. The area's first residents were Native Americans, followed by the French who founded the city of St. Louis in the 1760s.

Immigrants from Germany, Italy, Ireland, and Greece flocked here in the 1800s, and African Americans migrated here from the South after the Civil War.

Add to them people from Asia, Bosnia, the Middle East, and Latin America who've settled here in recent years. They've formed communities and brought with them traditional food

**FOOD**

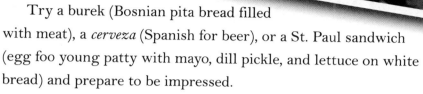

preparation techniques. The result is a Midwestern city where on any given day a person can sample food from around the world.

And that's just for lunch!

Try a burek (Bosnian pita bread filled with meat), a *cerveza* (Spanish for beer), or a St. Paul sandwich (egg foo young patty with mayo, dill pickle, and lettuce on white bread) and prepare to be impressed.

Entrepreneurs have established restaurants throughout the city, like Grbic (Mediterranean cuisine), Pho Grand (Vietnamese), Ranoush (Middle Eastern), and Meskerem (Ethiopian). Others have equipped food trucks to serve an endless array of epicurean delights. As Harry Karagiannis, a founder of the family-run Spiro's Greek Restaurants says, "Opa!"

# Fact BOX

From Rigazzi's signature fish-bowl beers (the jumbo, need-two-hands-to-hold glasses were patterned after 1904 World's Fair ice cream dishes) and Tony's award-winning cuisine and ambiance (Missouri's only AAA five-diamond award winner) to Spiro's saganaki (beer-battered, flamed kasseri cheese), St. Louis restaurants offer taste buds a chance to travel the world. And honestly, a night out at one of St. Louis's many delicious ethnic restaurants is considerably cheaper than a round-trip airline ticket.

# Brain on rye? With onions?

ONIONS

RYE

HOG BRAINS

HOT MUSTARD

**Brain food**

 FOOD

Ever hear of brain food? St. Louis has had that covered for decades. Does this food make you smarter? No clue. With a consistency like soft-cooked scrambled eggs, it is—quite literally—brains. Hog brains, to be exact.

Schottzie's Bar and Grill's Mike Carlson, fifteen-year veteran and son of co-owner Bob Carlson, says the secret's in the preparation and serving: "We flour and season the brains, shape them into patties, fry them, and serve them on rye with hot mustard, dill pickles, and red onions. People love them."

Brain sandwiches have long been a South St. Louis favorite. Their popularity dates back to the days of the Great Depression when nothing was wasted. Several restaurants offer them, like Fergie's Bar & Restaurant and the Crow's Nest, but Schottzie's reputation spread beyond St. Louis. Andrew Zimmern, host of television's *Bizarre Foods America*, brought his cameras to Schottzie's. "The age of brain sandwich customers is fifty-plus years," Carlson says. "But when that episode airs, we get a lot of younger people who want to try them."

Schottzie's sells fifteen to twenty brain sandwiches each week. The only thing that's changed is the type of brains used. After the mad cow disease scare a few years ago, beef brains were no longer available.

# Ravioli can be fried? Who knew?

## Toasted ravioli—only in St. Louis

**Toasted ravioli**

🍴 **FOOD**

Think of tiny pasta squares filled with a dab of ground meat, spinach, and spices. Coat the squares with bread crumbs and fry to a golden brown. That's toasted ravioli, and once you try one, you'll want more—lots more.

As with other St. Louis originals, such as gooey butter cake, toasted ravioli began as a mistake. Italian immigrants came to St. Louis more than a century ago and settled in a section of South St. Louis dubbed the Hill. They brought a strong work ethic and generations-old family recipes. Some opened restaurants.

The story goes that in the 1940s a chef accidentally dropped a few ravioli into hot oil instead of boiling water. Curiosity motivated the sampling of the fried, crunchy mistake, and they were declared delicious. Served with marinara sauce and Parmesan cheese, these small tasty pillows soon appeared on menus as "toasted" ravioli, and people loved them.

Several local restaurants claim to be the originators of toasted ravioli. "T-ravs are a St. Louis staple and we use the original recipe," says Charlie Gitto's restaurant employee Samantha Vogt. Owner Charlie Gitto has been featured on the Travel Channel detailing the time-consuming, multistep process his employees use to make the ravioli. And in case you're wondering, the restaurant sells about ten thousand ravioli each week. They're just that good.

# Pork steaks sound fancy, butt . . .

## The Lou's love of pork steaks

It's tough being the butt of jokes, but when something's this tasty, maybe that's not such a bad thing.

Stop by any St. Louis grocery store and look for pork steaks. You can't miss them. They're cheap, usually packaged to serve a crowd, and with lots of marbling—definitely not heart healthy.

 FOOD

But visit a grocery store outside the St. Louis area and you probably won't find them. Ask a butcher where the pork steaks are located and he or she will probably give you that blank look meaning, "I have no idea what you're talking about."

In reality, pork steaks aren't steaks at all. They're cut from the part of the pork shoulder often referred to as the Boston butt. But do give this economical local favorite a try. Slap those fat-marbled meat chunks on a hot grill, add a little seasoning, and listen to them sizzle. Cook, flipping occasionally until seared and no pink remains. If you're a fan of sauced pork, add another local favorite, Maull's barbeque sauce. Nothing says summer in St. Louis like pork steaks.

## Pork Steaks

# Another wedding, another plate of mostaccioli

 **FOOD**

It's been showing up at St. Louis wedding receptions for years. Not the cake or fruit punch. Not the creamy mints or nuts.

We're talking about mostaccioli—the dish made with a bit of ground beef, seasoned spaghetti sauce, and tube-shaped, Italian-inspired mostaccioli noodles. Highly economical, filling, and great for feeding crowds of distant relatives who show up for buffet dinners.

St. Louis has a sizable population of Italian descent, but this pasta dish isn't just served at Italian receptions. St. Louisans of all ethnicities enjoy a healthy serving or two of the stuff, often topped with a sprinkling of Parmesan cheese.

But if you want to taste really *good* mostaccioli, head to a restaurant like Zia's on the Hill and order the baked mostaccioli. Made with a hearty marinara sauce, melted Italian cheese, and Parmigiana, it's truly a taste of Italy.

# The slinger

St. Louis was home to legendary cookbook author Irma Rombauer (*The Joy of Cooking*), but her famous volume doesn't contain a recipe for the slinger.

Think late nights and early mornings, the craving for something greasy. Think about a combination of diner foods layered on one plate—eggs, hash browns, meat patty, and chili. And don't forget cheese, onions, jalapenos, and hot sauce on the side. That's the slinger—a St. Louis original.

JALAPENOS

ONIONS

CHEESE

CHILI

MEAT PATTY

HASHBROWNS

EGGS

**The Slinger**

**FOOD**

# *You really gonna eat that?*

"There's always been lots of hearsay about how the slinger came about," says Marji Rugg, daughter of Courtesy Diner owner Larry Rugg. "Dad says it's just always been around." Whatever its origin, generations of St. Louisans have feasted on this flavor amalgamation.

Some may wonder how anything with so many components can taste good, but those who eat them swear to the tasty appeal. "On weekends during third shift, we serve about 60 slingers each night," Rugg says. "During first shift, it can go as high as 150. And calorie count for a slinger is 1,300–1,500 calories." Don't plan on eating again for a while.

# Donut obsessed, perhaps?

The next time you crave a donut, give your mouth something to savor. St. Louis has several dozen locally owned and operated donut shops.

Terry Clanton, owner of World's Fair Donuts near the Missouri Botanical Garden, starts his work day at 4:30 a.m. He's been making donuts every day for the last forty years. Like his father before him, he takes pride in keeping his loyal customers supplied in donuts.

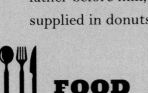

FOOD

"We make traditional donuts like cake, jelly, custard, and long johns," Clanton says. "We don't try to introduce new or unusual ingredient combos. We stick with what we do best and what our customers enjoy."

Some locals enjoy visiting small shops like Clanton's where the donuts are lined up like soldiers. Others call ahead with orders and pick them up at drive-through windows. Regardless of where they're purchased, it's difficult to find a bad donut in St. Louis. Low-calorie they're not, nor are they Paleo diet–compatible.

And then there's Strange Donuts. The company opened in 2013 and has locations in Maplewood and Kirkwood. Somewhat unconventional and altogether delicious, Strange Donuts features old-school favorites as well as donuts called "strangers." Strangers change frequently and feature unique and seasonal ingredients (think bacon).

And if you're one of those people who need to justify the consumption of multiple donuts, check out the mini donuts at the Soulard Farmers Market. Smaller donuts have fewer calories, so you can eat more than one, right? And what's not to love about a good local sugar high?

# How can cake be *gooey?*

**Gooey butter cake—a St. Louis specialty**

**FOOD**

It's one of those foods with a somewhat questionable background. Some say it was a mixing mistake. Others blame the order of ingredients. Regardless, it's a St. Louis tradition dating back to the early twentieth century that's loaded with calories but oh so delicious.

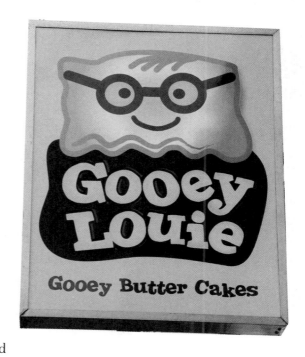

Gooey butter cake is often described as not really cake, custard, pie, or Danish, but a sweet confection that has elements of all of the above.

"It's a very traditional St. Louis item," says Talan Cooksey of Park Avenue Coffee, a Lafayette Square eatery specializing in gooey butter cake. "We have seventy-three official flavors, but traditional, triple chocolate, and white chocolate raspberry are our most popular flavors. We usually have eight or nine flavors available on any given day."

Park Avenue Coffee's gooey butter cakes are so popular they're carried in twenty St. Louis locations, including retail outlets and farmers markets. They've been featured on the *Today* show and the Food Network. Plus they're shipped throughout the world. "Gooey butter cakes are uniquely St. Louis," says Cooksey.

# Why are fish fries so popular in St. Louis?

**Meatless Friday cheats**

Who doesn't love a good local fish fry? All that yummy baked and fried fish, plus side dishes that can include shrimp, coleslaw, hush puppies, potatoes, bread, and a dessert. Perhaps not the best choice for the calorie conscious, but boy that's good eating.

The practice of eating fish instead of meat on Fridays has been observed by Catholics for two thousand years. And The Lou has a lengthy Catholic connection. The city was founded by French fur traders. When they first divided the riverfront land into lots, they designated a plot of ground for a Catholic church. That piece of land remains in the hands of the Archdiocese of St. Louis (established in 1826) and is home to the Basilica of Saint Louis, King of France (a.k.a. the Old Cathedral). Since then, hundreds of Catholic parishes have opened in the area.

Not surprisingly, Lenten fish fries are popular in the area. "Between seventy-five and a hundred fish fries are held in the Archdiocese of St. Louis during Lent," says Gabe Jones, archdiocese media relations specialist. "Fish fries are held in churches or places like Knights of Columbus facilities from Perryville, Washington, and Lincoln County to everyplace in between."

 **FOOD**

Archdioceses in other parts of the country have granted dispensations allowing parishioners to eat some semiaquatic animals as Friday meat substitutes. For example, in Detroit the archdiocese has

given muskrat a dispensation as an acceptable meat substitute. In Louisiana, alligator is acceptable. From time to time, rumors surface in the St. Louis area that due to its semiaquatic nature, beaver is an acceptable Lenten meat substitute. A local restaurant even serves beaver during the six weeks of Lent.

But according to Jones, "There are no dispensations for meat substitutes along those lines in the archdiocese of St. Louis." In other words, some folks may eat beaver as a meat substitute, but it isn't an acceptable substitute in the eyes of the archdiocese. Only one church, St. Peter Catholic Church in St. Charles, serves something in addition to fish during their Lenten fish fries. "You'll find frog legs on the menu at St. Peter, but only there." says Jones.

# Fact BOX

St. Louisans *do* love beer. And if you attend a fish fry sponsored by a local Catholic church or affiliated organization, chances are you'll be able to enjoy a cold brewski. "I can't definitely say whether or not all seventy-five-plus Catholic fish fries in the archdiocese serve some form of alcohol, because that's determined on a location-by-location basis," says archdiocese spokesperson Gabe Jones. "But it's safe to say that, by and large, most fish fries will serve beer and/or wine."

# Why do I feel like I'm in an outdoor sauna?

**The Lou's high humidity**

Clothing feels damp.
Skin feels sticky.
Mouth is dry.
Hair is frizzy.

WEATHER

24

| TEMPERATURE AND HUMIDITY. | 7 A.M. | 10·30 A.M. | 2 P.M. | 2·30 P.M. | 9 P.M. | |
|---|---|---|---|---|---|---|
| JANUARY 1, 1881: | | | | | | |
| Thermometer, degrees Fahr..... | 4 | 12 | 27·5 | 29·5 | 30 | 2 |
| Relative humidity, per cent..... | 74 | 61 | 76 | 73 | 68 | 7 |
| Actual humidity, grains........ | 0·44 | 0·59 | 1·35 | 1·35 | 1·35 | |
| JUNE 1, 1881: | | | | | | |
| Thermometer, degrees Fahr..... | 73 | 78 | 79 | 80 | 70 | 69 |
| Relative humidity, per cent..... | 72 | 61 | 54 | 51 | 80 | 85 |
| Actual humidity, grains........ | 6·36 | 6·46 | 5·95 | 5·76 | 6·41 | 6· |

Ah, summer in St. Louis. What is it about this landlocked part of the country that makes summertime so humid and uncomfortable?

"The Gulf of Mexico is the St. Louis region's primary source of humidity and heat in some part as well," says Jon Carney, meteorologist with the National Weather Service in St. Louis. "There's not much between us and the Gulf except for the Ozarks, and if we didn't have the Gulf, the Great Plains and Mississippi Valley would be a desert. The warmest days occur when there is a very large ridge of high pressure aloft accompanied by west or southwest wind blowing downslope from the Great Plains or Ozark Plateau. As air descends, it compresses and heats up.

"Also, agriculture in the region can add humidity locally through evapotranspiration."

But it's difficult to be happy when you walk outside and instantly break into a drenching sweat. Is St. Louis weather unusual? "Actually, no," says Carney. "Our weather is pretty typical for cities at our latitude and elevation above sea level."

# Is an earthquake really possible?

## New Madrid, the San Andreas of the Midwest

Shake, rattle, and roll. Anyone who's experienced a small earthquake or tremor can attest to a feeling of helplessness as the ground and everything attached to it moves.

Shortly after 2 a.m. on December 16, 1811, residents of tiny New Madrid, Missouri, felt the first tremor of a series of earthquakes. The earth opened with large fissures, the nearby Mississippi River generated tremendous waves, and thousands of trees, islands, and buildings were destroyed. A second, stronger earthquake occurred January 23, 1812, followed by a third on February 7, 1812. The quakes caused damage hundreds of miles away, including St. Louis. They were deemed the worst in U.S. history.

Since then, people living in southeastern Missouri have feared another severe earthquake. Infrequent small tremors serve as reminders of what could happen. Is an earthquake along the New Madrid fault a serious possibility?

**WEATHER**

"Yes, there are small earthquakes on the New Madrid fault all the time, usually several every month," says meteorologist Jon Carney. "They're small and we don't feel them way up here. If New Madrid ever cut loose with a really big earthquake, it would be a disaster."

## NEW MADRID

(Continued from other side)

The New Madrid Earthquake, made up of a series of monstrous and lesser shocks, which began Dec. 16, 1811, and continued over a year, centered here. One of the great earthquakes of the world because of severity and length it caused little loss of life in a thinly settled region. Some of the shocks were felt as far as 1100 miles. Reelfoot Lake across the river is a result of the disaster. New Madrid land certificates, good for public land elsewhere, were provided sufferers by U.S. relief act, 1815, which benefited mostly speculators.

In 1862 Union forces captured New Madrid and by means of a "canal" sawed through a submerged forest to a bayou, gained control of Island No. 10 and command of the river. Nearby in Mississippi Co. is Belmont battlefield, scene of an 1861 engagement in which both Federal forces under Grant and Confederates under Pillow claimed victory.

New Madrid, seat of government of one of 5 Spanish districts, later one of Missouri's first 5 counties, serves a farming community. Cotton and soybean crops predominate. Rich land has been reclaimed by the Little River and St. Johns Levee drainage systems.

Erected by State Historical Society of Missouri and State Highway Commission, 1953

# Auntie Em, why is everyone running to the basement?

## St. Louis—a severe weather magnet

People talk about St. Louis weather extremes. Temperatures can reach the seventies in January, and then it snows in April. Why such variations?

"From a forecaster's perspective, the weather here is unique because we sit in a region where we experience all four seasons," says meteorologist Jon Carney. "We have extremes primarily because of geography. There's not much between us and the Gulf of Mexico, and there's nothing between us and the Arctic except a few wire fences. Cold air masses can rush south with no geographical impediment, and warm air masses can rush north and east with very little geographical impediment. However, we're actually no more susceptible to severe weather than any other Midwestern/Great Plains city.

**WEATHER**

"We do have some bad floods though, and that's because about one quarter of the continental U.S. drains right past St. Louis on the Missouri and Mississippi Rivers," Carney continues. "That's a lot of water. Mostly St. Louis weather is mild but with a few days of extreme weather each year, which makes forecasting challenging. This is a great place to study the profession of meteorology."

**Fact BOX**

If the weather in St. Louis seems wetter and warmer than you remember in years past, it is. "Beginning in the early 1980s, an unprecedented wet period has evolved in Missouri," says Pat Guinan, University of Missouri Extension state climatologist.

"Over the past few decades, all four seasons have witnessed more above-normal precipitation years in Missouri, most notable in winter and spring. Missouri's most recent warm annual temperature trend began in the mid-1980s, and 2012 was the warmest year on record since 1895," Guinan continues. "Seasonally, Missouri winters and springs have experienced the greatest warming trend, and snowfall trends have been declining.

"Some of this warming effect is likely due to urbanization, and some of it is likely due to broad-scale climate change," says meteorologist Jon Carney.

# This so-called river is everywhere, but where's the water?

## The River des Peres, St. Louis's man-made waterway

Cruise the streets of southwestern St. Louis and you'll see it. Just over there is the River des Peres. Signs, paved basin, bridges, protective fencing. It's all there—but often no water. No cascading ripples. Not even a trickle. So why all the infrastructure for something that isn't?

 **WATER**

To truly understand the River des Peres (French for River of the Fathers), a small stream noted as early as the 1700s, it's necessary to travel back in St. Louis history.

Step back to the days of cesspools, standing rainwater, and flooded low-lying ground. In other words, to the days before the establishment of an underground sewer system for rainwater and other liquid wastes. St. Louis was smelly and unsanitary.

Wanting to impress visitors to the Louisiana Purchase Exposition (1904 World's Fair), politicians made decisions that would have a lasting impact on St. Louis. Channels were dug, water rerouted underground, and natural streams diverted to connect to what became an eighteen-mile-long channel and the backbone of St. Louis's sewer system.

The River des Peres seldom fills its designated path. In the summer, the outdoor sections become home to greenery, frogs, and turtles. The underground sections provide shelter for snakes and rats. But when the spring rains fall for days on end, the river-that-isn't can become raging floodwaters filled with fish from outlying tributaries. And only rarely (the flood of 1993) does the river overflow its man-made banks and flood surrounding areas. Most days the river is an ecological playground in an expansive concrete trench.

# The Mississippi River looks pretty brown and determined— like those big birds over there.

## Bald eagles and other migratory birds spend their winters in St. Louis.

Welcome to St. Louis—home of the Gateway Arch, the Cardinals, and migratory birds.

St. Louis sits near the confluence of three major waterways—the Mississippi, Missouri, and Illinois Rivers. Generations of humans found the location ideal for transportation and trade. Generations of migratory birds including eagles, Canada geese, ducks, snow geese, and swans found it's a great place to spend the winter.

"We're right on the Mississippi flyway," says Pat Behle of the Columbia Bottom Conservation Area, part of the Missouri Department of Conservation. "It's typical for migratory birds to follow the Mississippi north to south and south to north. They're looking for a place to eat and a place to rest. Water and vegetation, wetlands. We have them."

 **WATER**

Water near the rivers' dams is constantly churning. The surface doesn't freeze, making an assortment of fish readily available for hungry birds. Tall trees and bluffs near the rivers provide ideal lookout and roosting locations.

Most of the area's eagle sightings happen during January and February, but a few eagles remain year round, says Behle. "What makes St. Louis unique is that we have the confluence of these great rivers. It's the third or fourth largest watershed in the world, and these birds have been doing this forever."

# Fact BOX

Snowy owls ordinarily call the Arctic region home. The species is one of a handful that can tolerate the region's frigid winter temperatures. But in recent winters, a few young snowy owls have been spotted near St. Louis–area rivers. Wildlife experts speculate that they come south in search of food. The owls have no known predators. As their population continues to increase, their food supply may be running low. So for a few months, St. Louis bird-watchers can glimpse the majestic beauty of their pure white feathers and four-foot wingspan. Once temperatures warm here, the owls return north to breed.

# Waterworks Standpipes

Early water towers combined form and function.

Drive through the city of St. Louis and you'll probably see them. They're tall, thin, artistically crafted, and look totally out of place in today's world. Only seven of hundreds built in the United States a hundred-plus years ago remain. St. Louis is home to three of them, and they're listed on the National Register of Historic Places.

It was the end of the nineteenth century, and St. Louis was one of the largest U.S. cities. As the population grew so too did the demand for water. At that time, steam pumps sent water through residential and commercial buildings' pipes, but they weren't dependable for getting water to upper floors. To help control pressure surges in water pipes, large cities built vertical standpipes. Water rose and fell inside the standpipes and helped prevent surges. Decorative towers were built to conceal the pipes.

St. Louis's first standpipe water tower was built in 1871 on Grand Avenue. The Grand "Old White" tower is topped with decorative iron leaf work and remained in service until 1912. The Bissell "New Red" tower was built 1885–86 from red brick with terra-cotta and gray stone accents. It remained in use until 1912. The Compton Hill tower is the youngest of St. Louis's standpipes. Built in 1898, it was used until 1929. Through the years various factions supported tearing down the standpipes, but preservationists were successful in keeping the architectural relics intact.

# The St. Louis District of the U.S. Army Corps of Engineers—

# Important and Understated

**They keep things going.**

Ask a St. Louisan what the Corps of Engineers does in our area and you may get a blank stare. Corps activities seldom generate much press coverage, but the smooth functioning of the waterways in and around the St. Louis area is the direct result of Corps activities.

Missouri became the twenty-fourth state in 1821. Soon engineers began improving navigation of the Mississippi River at St. Louis. The river and its safe navigation were of utmost importance to the city. In the days before railroads, commerce and communication depended almost exclusively on nearby rivers. If St. Louis was going to become the next great city, rivers needed to be cleared of rocks, sandbars, uneven water flows, and snags.

 **WATER**

Snags were made up of tree branches, pieces of sunken boats, and other debris found floating in river currents. Deep snag piles often lurked just below the water's surface and were the cause of numerous boat disasters. With government funding, the Corps became responsible for clearing the river passage and improving its safety, thus aiding commerce. St. Louisans welcomed the help.

Through the years, the St. Louis District of the Corps has developed systems of levees, dykes, channels, sloughs, jetties, and dredges that have improved the navigation of the Mississippi River. The Corps also built dams and implemented flood control measures.

In addition to river engineering, the Corps is responsible for inspecting dams, wastewater management, environmental enhancement, urban water resource planning, flood protection (i.e., floodwalls), hydropower, responding to natural disasters, and outdoor recreation (places like Clarence Cannon Dam, Shelbyville Dam, Rend Lake, Carlyle Lake, and Alton Lock and Dam No. 26). In recent months, the Corps has been involved in ongoing cleanup of radioactive waste along St. Louis County's Coldwater Creek.

**Fact BOX**

The St. Louis District of the U.S. Army Corps of Engineers maintains a navigation channel nine feet deep and three hundred feet wide along three hundred miles of the Mississippi River between Saverton, Missouri, and Cairo, Illinois.

# More breweries than you can shake a stein at

A toast to nineteenth-century German immigrants who made St. Louis a leader in malt beverage production—and consumption. If not for their unhappiness in das fatherland, thousands might have stayed put. Instead, they heard about an idyllic place called Missouri and flocked here. They came to St. Louis in search of a new life. They arrived with few possessions, a strong work ethic, and family recipes for beer.

Breweries popped up all over town. St. Louisans quenched their thirsts with hometown brews like Budweiser, Falstaff, Griesedieck, Lemp's, ABC Bohemian, Hyde Park, Gast, and Schorr-Kolkschneider. Some lasted a short time. Others remain top sellers today. What was true then is true today—we love beer.

And imagine the brewers' delight when they discovered the convenience of caves spread beneath St. Louis. Think of it as natural refrigeration or bier storage, St. Louis style.

Some breweries were intentionally located near the underground caves. Industrious brewers reinforced them with stone and wood and built tunnels. Once artificial refrigeration arrived, the caves were no longer needed. Time passed and most

## DRINK UP

of them were lost or blocked due to aboveground development.

And St. Louisans' taste for all things beer hasn't diminished. The Gateway City is home to microbreweries, brewpubs, and regional craft breweries, including Urban Chestnut Brewing Company and the Saint Louis Brewery with Schlafly products.

A great opportunity to sample dozens of locally crafted brews happens each May. For twenty-plus years, Microfest has attracted those who enjoy producing—and drinking—beer. Attendees receive a souvenir glass and can have it filled (endlessly) with different dark, light, and flavored brews. Microfest most recently featured more than 120 different beverages. (FYI, portable restrooms are located nearby.)

Built on the foundations of the past with an eye to the future, today's St. Louis brewing industry thrives.

## Fact BOX

Missouri is nicknamed the Cave State. According to the Department of Natural Resources, Missouri has more than fifty-six hundred recorded caves. Some, like Meramec Caverns and Onondaga Cave, are show caves and are open to the public. Wild caves are located on private property. In 1980, the Missouri legislature passed the Cave Resources Act to protect caves from vandalism and trespassers.

# The ghosts of soft drinks past

Necessity is the mother of invention, or so an old saying goes. St. Louis is famous for beer. Generations downed our brews. That is, until the unfortunate inconvenience known as Prohibition. From 1920 to 1933, U.S. companies ceased malt beverage production.

Suddenly multitudes of people were without work. How would the local laborers who made glass bottles and wooden pallets, who handled raw materials and produced and distributed beer, support themselves and their families?

The answer was soft drinks.

Ingenious industry leaders repurposed materials and equipment to manufacture nonalcoholic, malt-free beverages. And workers were back on the job. Products like Howdy Orange, 7UP, Orange Smile, Whistle, Vess, and IBC Root Beer were born in St. Louis.

"The manufacture of soft drinks got people back to work," says Greg R. Rhomberg, lifelong St. Louis memorabilia collector, amateur local history buff, and owner of Antique Warehouse. "Besides, people needed something to mix with their illegally produced home brews and moonshine."

Traces of St. Louis's soft drink past remain visible. The Orange Smile Sirup Company building, located at Ninth and Soulard, has been repurposed for residential living. A somewhat faded twelve-foot Vess soda bottle stands near I-70 in downtown St. Louis. With its mid-twentieth-century

**DRINK UP**

40

graphics, it's a reminder of St. Louis's soft drink history.

And for the last twenty-plus years, Fitz's soft drinks have called St. Louis home. Fitz's may not have a global presence, but a taste of the company's locally produced flagship root beer or cream, orange, or cherry soda is a throwback to a different era. The drinks are crisp, flavorful, and sweetened with natural cane sugar. No high fructose corn syrup here.

Fitz's Root Beer began here in the 1940s but faded into obscurity. In 1993, tiny Fitz's Bottling Company opened in the Delmar Loop, featuring a vintage 1940s bottling machine and original product formulas. Then, as now, customers at the adjoining restaurant watch with fascination as a line of clean glass bottles snakes its way from empty to filled, capped, and ready for consumption. Bigger isn't necessarily better.

# Fact BOX

C. L. Grigg was an entrepreneur. He also knew how to keep a secret. Although many speculated about the origin of the name he gave his Depression-era lemon-lime soft drink, he never revealed it. The most frequent guess? The sparkling product got its name because it contained seven ingredients. Guess we'll never know for sure why the Uncola was called 7UP.

The flavor extract for 7UP is derived from oils taken from the outer peelings of fresh lemons and limes. The fruits' pulp, juice, and seeds are waste products.

# Anyone from here sleeping with the fishes?

*Best wishes of*

*Wᵐ J. Lemp Brewing Co.,*

**St. Louis's organized crime connection**

Once upon a time, St. Louis had connections to organized crime, specifically the Mafia.

Blame it on implementation in 1920 of the Eighteenth Amendment to the U.S. Constitution, prohibiting the manufacture, distribution, and sale of alcoholic beverages. Such restrictions in a city that loves its beer and spirits was bound to cause an uproar.

It's the principle of supply and demand. It wasn't long before enterprising underground networks took advantage of the opportunity to supply the demands of thirsty St. Louisans. Complex syndicates functioned here as well as in other major cities, including Chicago, Detroit, and, Cleveland.

"The Mafia had connections in St. Louis, but they are diminished now," said the late Robert Lowery Sr., former member of St. Louis's Major Case Squad and the St. Louis Strike Force on Organized Crime and former city of Florissant mayor. Lowery attributed the decline in the Mafia's St. Louis presence to successful law enforcement and younger generations not wanting to become involved.

# Hoosier?
# But I'm not
# from Indiana.

## The peculiar vocabulary of St. Louisans

**WHAT'S IN A WORD?**

Many places in the United States have them. They're words that by their mere utterance conjure images of a stereotype—and not necessarily a positive one.

In St. Louis, the word "hoosier" has nothing to do with the state of Indiana (those people are Hoosiers) or your grandmother's antique kitchen cabinet. To label someone a hoosier means the person can be classified based on certain stereotypical parameters.

For example, a St. Louis hoosier leaves the Christmas tree in the family room year-round, merely covering it with a sheet when it's not the holiday season. A St. Louis hoosier keeps plastic flowers in outdoor pots—even when the temperature is -10°F. Why? Because they look pretty and add a pop of color. Never mind that they're weighted down by six inches of snow. A St. Louis hoosier shops at the grocery store with a head full of pink plastic hair rollers but covers them with a colorful scarf and dons lipstick because she might run into someone she knows.

## You get the idea.

## Fact BOX

Various words are used in other parts of the country to describe the folks St. Louisans call hoosiers.

These include redneck, hayseed, local yokel, hick, good old boy, rural, country bumpkin, hillbilly, and backwoods.

45

Blame it on the French settlers of the 1760s. Or blame it on later immigrants who learned English as a second language.

Call it vernacular or folk vocabulary, St. Louis has unique word pronunciations. They start as mispronunciations and eventually become part of local speech. "Every major population center features regional and ethnic variants in pronunciation, grammar, or word choice," says University of Missouri–St. Louis's Dr. Benjamin Torbert. "St. Louis's combination of variants generally owes to its geography and history, different ethnic and linguistic inputs.

"St. Louis's language reflects its people, so we boast an array of influence," he continues. "This is a natural process—when speakers borrow a word from another language, they change it to fit their own language, somewhat."

In St. Louis, roof sounds like "ruff," wash and washed are pronounced "warsh" and "warsht," across is "acrost," "Dezember" sounds German, sandwich becomes "sammich," and a twenty-five-cent coin is pronounced "quater." Interstate 44 is pronounced "Farty-Far," and an ice cream sundae is pronounced "sunduh."

"I would say that most large U.S. cities have their own unique word pronunciations," says Washington University's Dr. Brett Hyde. "If they are large enough, they might have several distinct varieties."

*St. Louis Post-Dispatch* columnist Joe Holleman agrees. "New York does. Chicago does. They're neither right nor wrong. They're just uniquely that city, a different way of saying things.

"What's different about St. Louisans is that they apologize for their mispronunciations. New Yorkers don't apologize for anything"

# The Fourth City?

## What were the first three?

St. Louis, one of America's top cities

 **WHAT'S IN A WORD?**

Newspaperman Logan Uriah Reavis had big dreams following the Civil War. He wanted to make St. Louis one of the country's premier cities. He campaigned to have the nation's capital, including its buildings, relocated from Washington, D.C., to St. Louis. A national conference was held here and plans were discussed. Obviously the move never happened.

```
Rank Place                          Population
---------------------------------------------
   1  New York city, NY ........  3,437,202
   2  Chicago city, IL..........  1,698,575
   3  Philadelphia city, PA.....  1,293,697
   4  St. Louis city, MO........    575,238
```

The 1860 U.S. census showed St. Louis with a larger population than Chicago. But in 1856, Chicago opened the Chicago and Rock Island Railroad bridge across the Mississippi River, a move important to the city's commercial transportation and growth. St. Louis's Eads Bridge didn't open across the Mississippi until 1874. St. Louis leaders worried that the 1870 census would put Chicago's population ahead of St. Louis's. Not ones to let the truth stand in the way of a good story, they inflated the census figures.

But the 1880 census figures didn't lie. Chicago had the larger population.

Population growth in St. Louis continued. By 1900, St. Louis was indeed ranked the nation's fourth-largest city. And in 1904, the world came to St. Louis for the Louisiana Purchase Exposition, a world's fair like no other.

# How did I pass through eight cities in three miles driving down one road?

## St. Louis and the abundance of small municipalities

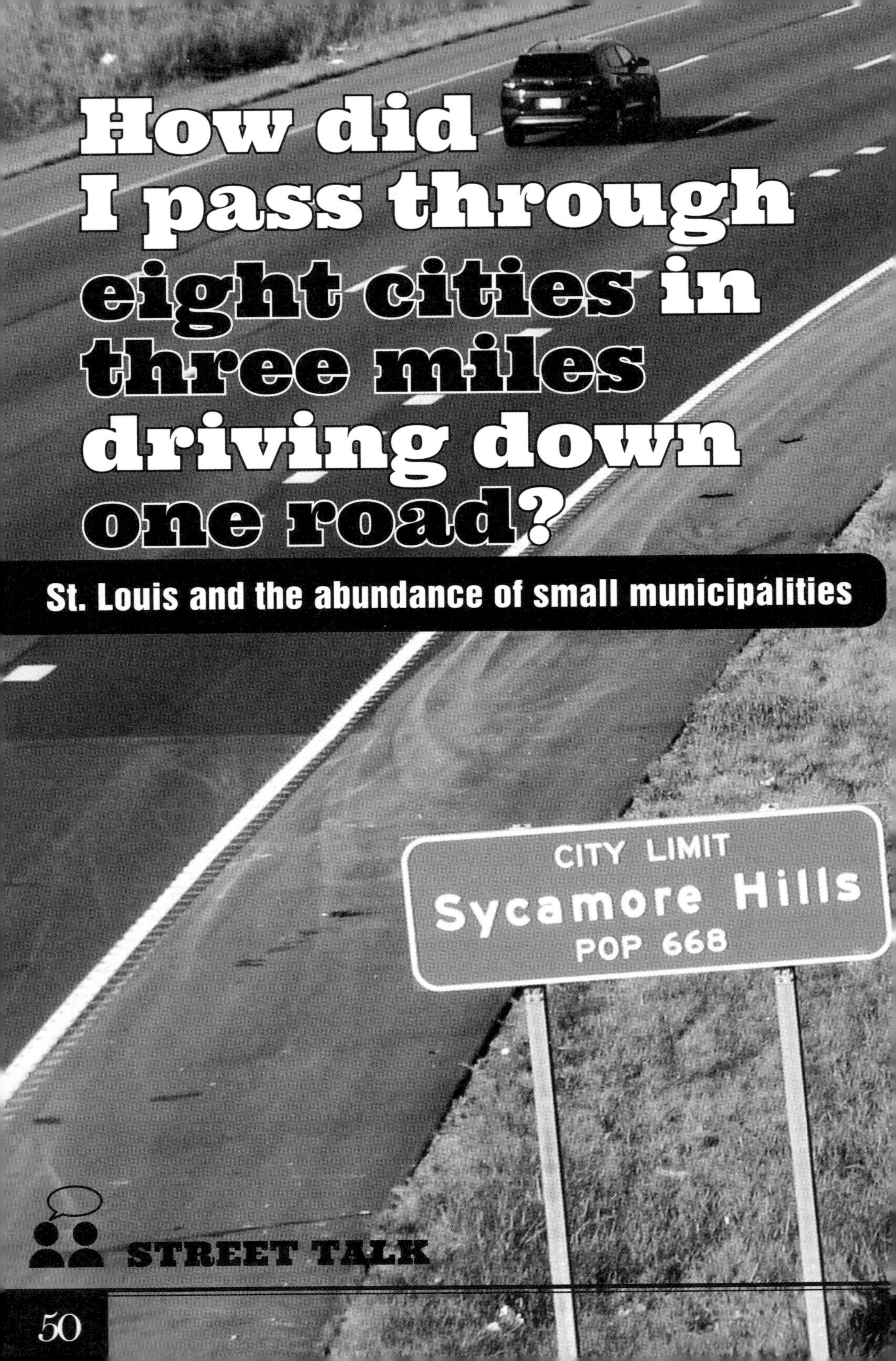

CITY LIMIT
Sycamore Hills
POP 668

STREET TALK

The city of St. Louis has some seventy-nine neighborhood areas, including private streets, historically renovated residences, and working-class and industrial sections. These include the Central West End, Soulard, Benton Park, Bevo Mill, Carondelet, Baden, the Hill, Penrose, O'Fallon, and Tower Grove East.

In 2018, St. Louis County contained eighty-eight municipalities, some of which are small and many of which have their own municipal services. These include Maplewood, Brentwood, Grantwood Village, Crestwood, and University City. In recent years, several municipalities have dissolved and merged with nearby areas.

Roads like Olive, Gravois, and Delmar run for miles, taking drivers from parts of the city of St. Louis and on through St. Louis County municipalities. Bound on the east by the Mississippi River, St. Louis grew and expanded north, south, and west from its original village settlement along the river.

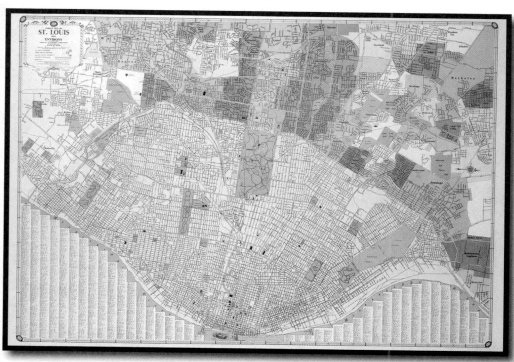

# The rolling stop—
## a St. Louis tradition

## How St. Louisans view stop signs

According to the St. Louis Department of Streets, the city has approximately one thousand miles of streets (not including hundreds of alleys). And if you ask drivers who live in or commute to the city, it contains about a million stop signs. At least it seems that way.

"In reality, the city has twenty-two thousand stop signs," says a department spokesperson. Contrary to what some drivers may think, stop signs aren't randomly placed at locations as an inconvenience. Stop signs, as well as all traffic control devices, have a purpose. Their purpose is to enhance traffic flow and improve safety for drivers as well as pedestrians.

St. Louis, like some other large metropolises, has a dense street grid. Major arterial roadways run through the city, intersected by hundreds of secondary and cross streets. Factors such as traffic and pedestrian volume, speed, high accident rates, and limited visibility are considered prior to stop sign installation.

 **STREET TALK**

However, some areas seem to have an excessive number of stop signs. Drivers can hardly accelerate before needing to brake again for another stop sign. Therefore, quick glances and reduced acceleration (but not complete stops) have become commonplace on St. Louis streets—a.k.a. the rolling stop.

As defined by ordinance 17.02.500 of the St. Louis, Missouri, Code of Ordinances, "'Stop' means the complete cessation from movement." Failure to do so can result in citations and fines. Something to keep in mind the next time you roll through a stop sign.

# Can you still get your kicks on Route 66?

## The Mother Road is still alive in St. Louis.

U.S. Route 66 has been the inspiration for songs, movies, and a television show. It was built at a time when automobiles enabled Americans to become a more mobile society. It connected Chicago, Illinois, to Santa Monica, California, and it didn't take long for it to become known as America's Main Street.

Route 66 traversed through small towns in eight states. Missouri was one of those states. Soon filling (gas) stations, diners, motor courts, merchants, and tourist sights popped up along the route.

Route 66 in Missouri began in the late 1920s. It was

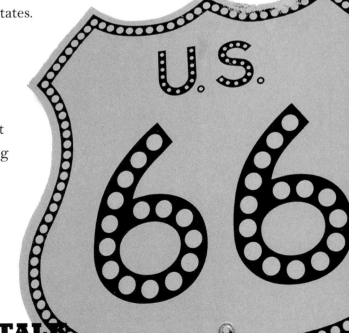

 **STREET TALK**

formed by piecing together decades-old trade and stage coach trails. It went up and down hills, around curves and beside scenic views. It came through the city of St. Louis and included parts of existing city streets (Grand, Delmar, Lindell, Boyle). It has been realigned numerous times through the years.

Although U.S. Route 66 has been decommissioned, original sections of it remain in the St. Louis area. St. Louis lawyer Norma M. Bolin conducted extensive research into the history of Route 66 after watching the movie *Cars*. The movie piqued her interest in the Mother Road. "The road continued to evolve in St. Louis, and some of the decades-old original structures still exist," she says. "I've read up on it and fell in love with the mom-and-pop operations along it. I decided if I didn't get this information down, it was going to be lost."

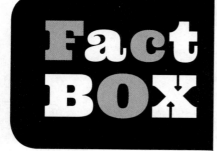

Seattle, Washington, claims to have been the location for the first gas station in 1907. However, St. Louis was the location of the first filling station in 1905. The St. Louis station offered drive-through refueling services for the increasingly popular automobile.

The first paving in Missouri happened in 1932 along part of St. Louis's Watson Road. Soon that section of roadway was incorporated into U.S. Route 66.

# Cherokee Street
## (more than a people, more than a tribe)

**A popular St. Louis street and neighborhood**

FURNITURE
SINCE 1894

OPEN

STREET TALK

French settlers established a village here in the 1760s and called it St. Louis. A grid pattern was established with streets named for trees and U.S. presidents, and in South St. Louis some were named for Native American tribes and rivers.

One such thoroughfare was Cherokee Street. With the arrival of electric streetcar lines in the 1890s, Cherokee Street became a residential and commercial hub. Dry goods and furniture stores, tailors, doctors, butchers, and milliners were there, as well as photography studios, barbershops, and saloons. No need to travel downtown.

The demise of streetcars and the popularity of automobiles and suburban shopping centers took a toll on Cherokee Street in the last half of the twentieth century, but today it is again a thriving destination. "Four dense, diverse neighborhoods surround Cherokee Street and are filled with passionate people engaged in their communities," says Cherokee Street liaison Anne McCullough. "Community here means business owners, artists, residents, and property owners invested in each other, committed to supporting inclusivity and diversity.

"Cherokee Street really has everything one might need—groceries, furniture, coffee, live music, art, pet shops, galleries, salons, barbershops, beer, office space, clothing, flowers, and plants."

**Fact Box**

South St. Louis streets named for Native American tribes and rivers include Potomac, Winnebago, Keokuk, Miami, Osage, Pontiac, Gasconade, Shenandoah, Powhatan, Hiawatha, Susquehanna, and Osceola.

# Why are St. Louis's downtown streets named for trees?

**Walnut**

**An arborist's delight**

**CHESTNUT ST**

**OLIVE ST**

**Spruce ST**

 **STREET TALK**

It was 1764. Pierre Laclede, his lieutenant Auguste Chouteau, and thirty men settled on the banks of the Mississippi River and began to build a trading village. The tiny settlement had three north-south streets and three east-west streets. Being of French descent, the settlers naturally gave the streets French names: The north-south streets were named La Grande Rue, Rue d'Eglise, and Rue des Granges. The east-west streets were named La Rue de la Tour, Rue de la Place, and Rue Missouri.

The streets were still known by their French names until 1809. From that time until 1826, the east-west streets were known by letters of the alphabet, along with a North or South prefix. In 1826, the city of St. Louis adopted the street-naming system originated by the city of Philadelphia. North-south streets were given number names (First, Second). East-west streets were named for trees (Chestnut, Walnut).

## Fact BOX

**Time passed. The names of some of the tree streets were changed to honor important individuals from St. Louis's early years. Hazel became Chouteau, Cherry became Franklin, Mulberry became Gratiot, Willow became Biddle, Plum became Cerre, and Myrtle became Clark.**

# Riding the Rails

## Railroading in St. Louis

St. Louis was a commerce center long before railroads. Its proximity to the Mississippi, Missouri, and Illinois Rivers, plus its location near the center of the country, made it an ideal transportation crossroads.

Railroads in Missouri were discussed as early as 1836, but construction of iron railroads didn't begin in St. Louis until 1851. Plans included small operations and multiple connector routes. The Eads Bridge, completed in 1874 and the first to span the Mississippi River, changed railroading in St. Louis. It and other railroad bridges made St. Louis a focal point of cross-continent commerce. Previously, freight was unloaded from trains onto ferries to cross the rivers and then reloaded onto trains.

In 1889, multiple railroads joined together to form the Terminal Railroad Association of St. Louis (TRRA). "TRRA was formed to construct and control railroad facilities and operations for the benefit of the owning railroads," says Ronald N. Zimmer, a fifty-year veteran of railway and waterways engineering and Museum of Transportation volunteer. "The role of the TRRA has been to transfer railcars from one railroad's yard to another's, providing interchange services. TRRA exists today."

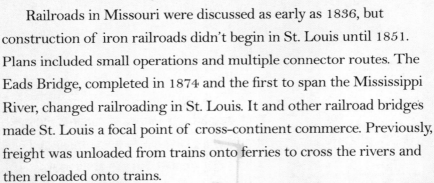

 **STREET TALK**

"Railroads may be as strong today as at any time in the past, both here and throughout the nation, but the nature of their business has changed," says Ronald N. Zimmer. "Almost all trackage in the St. Louis area is in fairly intensive use. However, the manner of use has changed. Door-to-door rail service for manufactured items is rarely economical today and lacks flexibility. This system has been replaced by containers (trailer bodies of typical highway trucks) that are loaded at factories, driven to rail yards, loaded on trains for long-distance trips, and then driven to their final destination. Containers hold a wide variety of manufactured goods such as electronics and garments. Trains in the St. Louis area also carry a lot of coal and sometimes windmill generator components, including 150-foot-long blades." Railroads operating in the St. Louis area today include the Union Pacific, BNSF, CSX, Norfolk Southern, Kansas City Southern, TRRA, and Amtrak. Several small railroads serve specific industrial areas.

The TRRA was also responsible for building Union Station, which opened in 1894. "Union Station provided for all passenger activity at a single location since St. Louis was a termination point for all railroads," says Zimmer. "If your destination was not St. Louis, you could transfer from one train to another without moving to another station. Compare this with Chicago, which had at least five railroad stations, each serving a different group of railroads."

By the 1940s, approximately one hundred thousand passengers a day passed through Union Station on their way to or from a train. Union Station was designated a National Historic Landmark in 1976 and was restored in 1985.

# I'm on Lindbergh Blvd., wait North Kirkwood Road, wait Lindbergh? And why isn't one Watson enough?

## St. Louis streets and unexpected name changes

What's in a street name? Apparently a lot. And in St. Louis, names change.

It was a big deal when James P. Kirkwood brought the Pacific Railroad to St. Louis in 1850. Now people could live in outlying areas and commute to work in St. Louis.

Suburban St. Louis living was born in 1853 with the founding of Kirkwood, the first planned residential community west of the Mississippi River. It was common at that time to name streets for U.S. presidents. "Except Kirkwood residents didn't like Presidents Tyler and Polk," says Sue Burkett, Kirkwood Historical Society librarian. "They decided to name Kirkwood's main thoroughfare for American statesman Daniel Webster."

Webster Avenue existed in Kirkwood for more than sixty years. It was called Denny Road north and south of Kirkwood's city limits.

 STREET TALK

Then people complained that Webster Avenue and Webster Groves, a nearby suburb, were sometimes confused by railroad commuters. So in 1915, Webster Avenue became Kirkwood Road. The sections north and south of Kirkwood remained Denny Road.

Charles Lindbergh became a hero in 1927 following his historic nonstop flight across the Atlantic Ocean. City officials wanted to recognize his St. Louis connection, so in 1930 the Denny Road sections became Lindbergh Boulevard. But some residents were unhappy. A group fought unsuccessfully to have the Denny name reinstated. "Or so the story goes," says Burkett.

And you've heard of Route 66, but what about Route 366?

In 1979, U.S. Route 66, America's Mother Road and the connection between the East and West Coasts, was decertified between Joplin, Missouri, and Chicago, Illinois. The Missouri Department of Transportation then became responsible for

upkeep of the Show-Me State's share of the roadway. After modifications and rerouting, the roadway was renamed Missouri Route 366. And to add to the confusion, sections of Route 366 passing through St. Louis were known locally as Chippewa Street and Watson Road.

Street name changes are not uncommon here and elsewhere, Burkett says. "Street name configurations change in many areas due to societal conventions and expansion."

# Why are there so many one-way streets in St. Louis?

**But I was only going one way.**

St. Louis streets trace their origins back to Pierre Laclede and the settlers who established a village here in the 1760s. "This settlement will become one of the finest cities in America," Laclede predicted.

Early structures, including a fur trading house, were located near the river on land that's now part of the Gateway Arch grounds. The trading house became the center of the village and the origination point from which all measurements were taken for locating lot divisions and streets. The village initially contained three north-south and three narrower east-west streets (dirt lanes) measuring thirty to thirty-six feet across.

Decades passed, and true to Laclede's prediction, the city grew and expanded. Additional lots, common fields, and streets were measured off as the town plat grew to

## STREET TALK

accommodate the increasing population. Old city maps show that most streets measured sixty feet right-of-way.

Once automobiles replaced wagons and streetcars, the streets became too narrow to safely accommodate two-way traffic. In 1923, bond issue funds were approved to help spruce up downtown St. Louis. Many of the narrow streets were converted to one-way traffic. Major thoroughfares like Olive and Market Streets were widened to accommodate multiple traffic lanes.

Street changes have been made in conjunction with construction of new stadiums and the convention center, but little else has changed with St. Louis street configurations.

# What's in a name?

Want to understand why certain names were given to streets and sections of St. Louis? Take a look at history books, said noted historian Norbury L. Wayman of the St. Louis Community Development Agency.

In 1826, St. Louis adopted a street-naming system originated by the city of Philadelphia. North-south streets were given number names. East-west streets were named for trees.

The century progressed and the St. Louis population grew. Additional land was platted and development spread from the original downtown village. Streets often were named for land owners or prominent St. Louisans. Henry Shaw's gift of land for a botanical garden resulted in street names such as Shaw, Flora, Botanical, and Tower Grove. Other street names utilized during that time read like a Who's Who of St. Louis. Geyer, Russell, LaSalle, and Lafayette honor notable St. Louis residents or historic figures. State names as well as the names of U.S. presidents and Indian tribes were popular street name choices.

 **STREET TALK**

Time passes. Some street names have been changed to recognize achievements of more contemporary individuals or the rich cultural heritage of immigrant populations. But names like Bremen, DeBaliviere, Wells, Baden, Kenrick, Bevo, Marquette, Shenandoah, Bellefontaine, Vandeventer, Bissell, and Cherokee harken back to people and places of yesteryear.

# Fact Box

Anti-German sentiment ran high during World War I. St. Louis, with its large German population, wasn't exempt. In the name of patriotism, street names with German origins were changed here and in other large cities. Von Versen Avenue became Enright Avenue, Kaiser Street became Gresham, and Berlin Avenue became Pershing Avenue (in honor of Missouri-born general John Pershing). In recent years, individuals affiliated with German American heritage groups have placed commemorative signs on some streets noting their original names.

PARKING FOR GERMANS ONLY

ALL OTHERS WILL BE TOWED

CITY ORD. 1145

HAMBURG AVE

# Urban blight becomes eclectic delight.

## Rebirth of the University City Loop

Sometimes it takes just one person with a vision to get things moving. Such was the case with entrepreneur Joe Edwards, the pony-tailed pied piper of University City.

Edwards returned to St. Louis, his hometown, after college. He and his wife, Linda, decided to open a small music-themed restaurant/bar along Delmar Boulevard in the part of University City called the Loop. The Loop had been a shopping and entertainment mecca in the first half of the twentieth century, but it fell out of favor as suburbia crept further west from downtown St. Louis.

Edwards quickly determined that his business wouldn't be successful unless the Loop area changed for the better. So began his one-man campaign to renew and rejuvenate an area that had once been vital. Original buildings with graceful architectural details remained. The area just needed some TLC and for others to see the economic potential. So Edwards got to work, forming committees to address things like lighting, sanitation, and security.

 **STREET TALK**

Blueberry Hill restaurant became a popular destination. The food was great, the beer cold, and the live entertainment excellent. Plus Edwards's amazing collection of ephemera and items from his childhood spoke to the memories of people throughout the St. Louis area.

In the 1980s, he created another attraction outside Blueberry Hill—the St. Louis Walk of Fame. Patterned after the Hollywood Walk of Fame, St. Louis's Walk has expanded to both sides of the street and pays homage to more than 140 famous St. Louisans.

And the revitalization continued. In 1995, Edwards bought and restored the nearby 1924 Tivoli Theatre. In 2000, he opened the Pageant, a performance venue. He opened Pin-Up Bowl in 2003 and the Moonrise Hotel, a boutique luxury hotel, in 2009. His latest projects include Peacock Loop Diner and the 2.2-mile trolley track that connects the Loop to St. Louis's crown jewel, Forest Park.

Gradually businesses and consumers returned to University City. Today the Loop is a destination for shopping, dining, and relaxing. Boutiques, unique shops, and local restaurants fill the once-vacant storefronts. Outdoor dining and street performers add to the ambiance of this thriving area. And it all started with the vision of one person.

# Fact BOX

Delmar Boulevard runs through the heart of University City and is sometimes called The Loop. This nickname harkens back to the twentieth century when cars and trucks shared St. Louis–area streets with streetcars. Streetcars arriving in U. City made a loop to turn around and head to other parts of town. With the advent of the recently created Loop Trolley Transportation District, University City has, so to speak, come full circle as a streetcar destination.

# Do you believe in ghosts?

## Ghost signs of St. Louis

Maybe you've seen them. Drive through St. Louis and notice the walls of some of the city's old brick buildings. They may be faded and difficult to decipher, but they're there. Before the days of billboards and neon and electric signs, advertisements were painted on the exterior walls of buildings. These faded but still somewhat visible images today are called ghost signs, and they're remnants of early St. Louis outdoor advertising.

Nineteenth-century businesspeople were savvy. Businesses were flexing their marketing muscles and stretching advertising dollars more than a century ago. They realized that not just any building would do. High visibility was important. Advertising signs were painted on buildings thought to have the greatest pedestrian, carriage, train, and later automobile traffic.

The more times the advertisements were seen, the better and more cost-effective the advertisements.

In reality, the businesspeople paying to have the products and services advertised on building walls probably had something temporary in mind. They might be amazed that the bold letters and graphics advertising things like flour, tobacco, buggies, stove polish, patent medicines, and beverages would still be visible more than a hundred years later. Such was the advantage of yesteryear's lead-based paints.

Individuals who painted wall advertisements were called walldogs. This was before OSHA regulations regarding workplace hazards, safety equipment, and eight-hour workdays. Walldogs worked tirelessly from the tops of ladders while juggling paint cans and brushes. They were artists whose skills were in demand as they traveled throughout the country.

Perhaps nineteenth-century wall advertising wasn't such a novel idea. Humans have been drawing and painting on cave walls throughout the world for tens of thousands of years.

# Why are there pieces of **metal track** in South St. Louis that lead nowhere?

## The tracks to nowhere

St. Louis's first streetcar was pulled by horses—functional but not speedy. Later, cars were conveyed by pulleys and electricity. St. Louis's extensive streetcar system had hundreds of cars and was one of the country's largest. Pieces of track peeking from beneath layers of paved street surfaces and leading from nowhere to nowhere are vestiges of that once-booming rail system.

Before the popularity of automobiles, passengers could travel from Wellston and Kirkwood to Creve Coeur Park and all points in between. Streetcars crossed the bridges to Illinois. Car transfers were easy as routes were marked. Overhead signs displayed destinations.

Decades passed. Streetcars and vehicles shared roadways. In the 1950s, streetcars took a back seat to individual vehicle ownership. Ridership decreased even further by the mid-1960s, and streetcars ceased running.

Lifelong St. Louis resident Mark Goldfeder grew up riding streetcars. His family owned a business near the Wellston Loop streetcar hub. Mark was a passenger on the last day of streetcar service in St. Louis— May 21, 1966.

 **STREET TALK**

"I was fifteen," Goldfeder says. "The *Post-Dispatch* gave away tickets, and a friend and I got some. We rode on that very last day. What an experience!"

Goldfeder's streetcar love never waned. He can name route numbers, intersecting streets and stops, and is the unofficial keeper of all things related to St. Louis streetcars, from clippings to home movies.

"At one time, St. Louis had nineteen streetcar companies," he continues. "Often the old tracks were just paved over. Street Department crews never know what they'll find when they start digging up the older streets to find water lines. And sometimes pieces of track simply pop through the pavement."

## Fact BOX

Streetcars have returned to St. Louis. Joe Edwards, University City's entrepreneur extraordinaire and developer of all things cool and retro, has been the driving force behind the reintroduction of a streetcar line in The Lou. The new streetcar route travels between the famed U. City Loop and the Missouri History Museum in Forest Park. Repurposed streetcars carry passengers through the heart of St. Louis. We're living in the twenty-first century's second decade, but familiar sounds like clanging streetcar bells are a welcome reminder of a simpler time.

# Soulard Farmers Market

It's difficult to describe Soulard Farmers Market. It's been a mainstay on Carroll Street since widow Julia Soulard donated land for a market in 1838. But it's so much more than a large brick building and open-air stalls. Let's just say it's a place you have to visit to understand.

A "Welcome Locavores" sign greets visitors. See the colorful rows of fresh and organic fruits and vegetables. Hear vendors calling out the day's meat specials (including alligator). Smell the fresh roasted nuts and exotic spices from the on-site spice shop.

 **TREASURES**

Taste samples of cheese, black grapes, homemade apple butter and jellies, and local wild honey. Touch the details of handcrafted jewelry and apparel, the soft fur of domestic animals (rabbits and chickens), and the creamy smoothness of handmade soap. Soulard Farmers Market is a place to be experienced with all five senses.

The market is open year-round, Wednesday through Sunday. Some vendors, like Schweiger's Produce, have been selling at the market for generations. Other vendors are newcomers to the market scene.

Stay an hour. Stay all day. There's plenty to see, do, eat, and drink at Soulard Farmers Market, including a pocket park, fresh mini-donuts, and beer. Plus it's a great place to people-watch. Observing local chefs selecting items for special dinner entrées is particularly intriguing.

Even if you don't plan to buy anything, chances are you'll want to bring cash and a few shopping bags for those items you discover you simply can't live without. FYI: Visitors rarely leave empty-handed.

# How did so many museums end up so close to each other?

## St. Louis's abundance of free museums

The Metropolitan Zoological Park and Museum District was established to oversee the tax-supported finances of five top-notch St. Louis cultural institutions: the Saint Louis Zoo, the Saint Louis Art Museum, the Saint Louis Science Center, the Missouri Botanical Garden, and the Missouri History Museum.

TREASURES

Establishment of the Zoo-Museum District (ZMD) in 1972 was an affirmation of support by citizens of both the city of St. Louis and St. Louis County, a guarantee that these institutions will continue to provide enriching experiences for residents and visitors both now and in the future. "I think the Zoo-Museum District is very effective," says one of eight ZMD commissioners.

## "It works for St. Louis and St. Louis County. We have five of the finest venues in the country in St. Louis."

Four of the five institutions are located in Forest Park. The Missouri Botanical Garden is located a few miles south of Forest Park. And the best thing about them? Free or minimal admission for everyone.

# City Museum

**One person's trash is another's treasure.**

There's a place in St. Louis where the building never stops. A place where items once thought to be trash have been functionally repurposed. A place so unique, so quirky, and oh-so-much fun for all ages. Welcome to City Museum!

Artist Bob Cassilly had the idea for a one-of-a-kind museum filled with architectural cast-offs and reclaimed visual oddities

collected throughout St. Louis. And because some of the items he collected were huge (airplanes, a log cabin, bridges, and a school bus), he needed plenty of room for visitors to play and explore. With the help of additional artists, he began construction of a museum like no other. In 1997, he opened City Museum in part of a former shoe warehouse with more than six hundred thousand square feet.

City Museum continues to grow and expand. A skateless skate park and a Ferris wheel, a series of man-made caves and a tree house, an aquarium and a ten-story slide, a vault room and miles of mosaics add to the fun. MonstroCity and the museum's rooftop provide places to explore as well as catch fabulous elevated views of downtown St. Louis.

# This  ZOO is a pretty big deal, isn't it?

## St. Louis's world-class zoo

Lions, tigers, and bears. Fish, reptiles, and insects. The ninety-acre Saint Louis Zoo is home to more than 560 species of animals, some rare and endangered. But it's not just the animals and state-of-the-art exhibits that make it a world-class zoo. "We work in conjunction with about 180 zoo partners and conservation organizations to focus on assessing animal health, sustaining habitats, wildlife management, breeding endangered species, education, and research," says a Saint Louis Zoo spokesperson.

Establishing a zoological park in Forest Park was a lengthy process. Forest Park opened in 1876. A small collection of animals from the city's Fairgrounds Park was purchased in 1891. In 1904, a domed walk-through flight cage was built by the Smithsonian Institution for the World's Fair. The cage was to be disassembled, but it was so popular that the city of St. Louis bought it in 1905 for $3,500.

 **TREASURES**

In 1910, citizens organized the Zoological Society of St. Louis. In 1913, the city set aside seventy-seven acres for a zoological park in Forest Park, with a Zoological Board of Control. The society incorporated as an independent civic organization in 1914. In 1916, citizens voted to tax themselves to pay for construction of the Saint Louis Zoo, becoming the first city in the world to do so.

"St. Louis has the unique distinction of being one of only three accredited zoos in the world that is free for everyone," says the zoo spokesperson. "It was created for St. Louisans by St. Louisans."

# Fact BOX

The Saint Louis Zoo has more than 18,700 wild animals, including thousands of ants, butterflies, and leaf-cutters. The zoo has 330 full-time employees and approximately 800 seasonal part-time employees to care for its residents. Each year the zoo attracts approximately three million visitors. It recently was voted America's best zoo and America's top free attraction.

# Does that building really mean NO HARM to our planet?

**James S. McDonnell Planetarium at the Saint Louis Science Center**

To some, it's that building near the zoo resembling a spaceship. Others notice the huge bow and colored lights during the holidays. In reality, it's the James S. McDonnell Planetarium, part of the Saint Louis Science Center.

TREASURES

The Planetarium dates to the early 1960s when space exploration was a hot topic. St. Louis's McDonnell Aircraft, important in the manufacture of the *Mercury* and *Gemini* space capsules, provided finances to construct a center for learning about and observing space. Famed local architect Gyo Obata designed the hyperboloid structure that opened to the public in 1963.

"It's a great resource for the city," says Bill Kelly, senior educator at the Planetarium. "It's a place for enthusiasts to learn more about astronomy. Schools can use visits here to supplement science curriculum. We have presentations about the night sky, constellations, galaxies, Mars, and the solar system. Plus our theater gives a very realistic night-sky experience."

The Planetarium, once owned by the city of St. Louis, was sold to the Saint Louis Science Center in the 1980s. A new science center opened in 1991 and featured a glass bridge over the highway to connect the two buildings.

Public nighttime sky watching is held every first Friday of the month in conjunction with the St. Louis Astronomical Society. "We bring out portable telescopes, and with the curvature of the Planetarium's roof, a lot of the artificial light from the city is cut out," Kelly says. "People can come, ask questions, and learn. We have about 150–200 in attendance, even on cold nights.

**Fact Box**

Gyo Obata graduated from Washington University. His designs can be seen throughout the world and in numerous St. Louis office buildings. He designed the Saint Louis Zoo's Children's Zoo and Living World and was involved with the renovation of Union Station.

THOMAS JEFFERSON

# What's that building that looks like a cross between a bird's nest and a jungle gym?

## The Climatron, a unique St. Louis structural gem

Buckminster Fuller was a twentieth-century inventor and innovator. The introduction of his unique geodesic dome structures in the 1950s generated much interest. With Fuller's dome design in mind, the Missouri Botanical Garden set out to build a greenhouse with no interior supports. It would be the first use of Fuller's design as a greenhouse and its construction would coincide with the garden's one hundredth anniversary.

TREASURES

"The Missouri Botanical Garden was trying to look to the future, to find a new symbol for the second hundred years," says Missouri Botanical Garden archivist Andrew Colligan. "The goal was to capture the public's imagination."

The Climatron's dome was built of Plexiglas and was intended to last five to ten years. It successfully attracted attention, but it leaked from the beginning. Renovations began in 1988 and included replacing the half-inch-thick Plexiglas with three-quarter-inch-thick tempered glass. The new panes were heavier, so an exoskeleton was built above the existing structure to support the additional weight. The Plexiglas was then removed.

"None of the other Fuller-inspired domes in the U.S. are exactly like this one," says Colligan. "It was the first of its kind and the only dome in the St. Louis area."

# Fact BOX

"Attendance at the garden was down in the 1950s because nothing was new," says Colligan. "The space industry started up at this time, and the dome looked like it was from outer space. There was no admission fee then for the garden. The Climatron opened in October 1960 with a fifty cents per person admission fee, and attendance soared. Twice as many visitors (four hundred thousand) came to the garden that year, even with the admission charge. It was a shot in the arm. It turned the garden around financially with the new funding generated by the dome."

# Singing the Blues

## The National Blues Museum calls St. Louis home.

St. Louis is home to some amazing cultural and civic institutions. The April 2016 opening of the National Blues Museum downtown marked the addition of another cultural gem, this one recognizing the American music form known as the blues.

Blues music has roots in social and economic oppression, hard times, and love gone wrong. It is unique in that it doesn't follow traditional musical form and expresses raw emotion in its beats and lyrics. The late singer Ray Charles once said, "Everybody can understand the blues."

"This is the only blues museum dedicated to telling the story of the blues locally, nationally, and internationally," says museum spokesperson Jacqueline Dace. "The goal is for the museum to be the premier entertainment educational resource focusing on the blues as the foundation of American music."

Some blues historians believe the blues originated in the Mississippi Delta and followed the mass migration of African Americans north after the Civil War. Many of those who left the area settled or performed in St. Louis as they headed north, bringing their unique music form with them. Composer W. C. Handy is credited with popularizing blues music. He wrote the song "St. Louis Blues" in 1914 and said, "The blues come

 **TREASURES**

from want, from desire, longing." Most American music forms introduced since then, including rock and roll, trace their origins to the blues.

The National Blues Museum has been in the works for several years. It includes a performance area for musicians called the Lumiere Place Legends Room, where limited-engagement shows will be scheduled. An item of interest currently at the museum is a loaned guitar, an original Lucille, from the B. B. King Museum in Indianola, Mississippi.

## Fact BOX

St. Louis was the home of an innovative blues style in the 1920s. Noted blues musicians of that era included Lonnie Johnson, Henry Townsend, and female vocalists Eva Taylor and Alice Moore. More recent St. Louis blues musicians include Miles Davis, Tina Turner, and Fontella Bass.

# A big stainless steel parabola

## The Gateway Arch

It was 1948. The city of St. Louis wanted to recognize Thomas Jefferson's part in the historic Louisiana Purchase and the city's role as the gateway to westward expansion in the United States. A competition was announced for the design of a symbolic monument to be built in downtown St. Louis.

A design submitted by Finnish-born, American-educated architect Eero Saarinen was selected. Sleek and unadorned, his design was symbolic of the city's place as the starting point for settlers headed west. When completed, the inverted stainless-steel catenary curve or arch would stand 630 feet high, more than twice the height of the Statue of Liberty, and would overlook the mighty Mississippi River.

But construction did not begin for years. Unfortunately, Saarinen died in 1961 before the monument was built. His office supervised the construction that was completed in October 1965.

The Arch is a modern marvel. Foundations for its two legs were placed sixty feet into the ground. The stainless-steel frame was designed to withstand strong winds as well as earthquakes. And small elevator cars carry visitors to the top center of the monument and its observation windows. Routine cleaning of the Arch's exterior keeps it looking bright and shiny for the millions of visitors it welcomes annually.

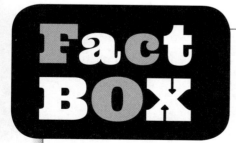

**Fact BOX**

**Eero Saarinen had a connection to another modern architectural marvel— the spectacular Sydney Opera House in Australia. A selection jury for the Sydney Opera House commission discarded several designs, including one submitted by architect Jorn Utzon. Saarinen looked through the discarded designs, recognized the merit in Utzon's unique design, and convinced the jury to select it. Saarinen also designed Washington, D.C.'s Dulles International Airport and the iconic Tulip chair.**

# A Witness to History

## The Old Courthouse

If walls could talk, those of the Old Courthouse near the riverfront could fill volumes.

The building began its life in 1826, a time when St. Louis's population was less than five thousand. It was known as the county courthouse for fifty years before the city of St. Louis and St. Louis County became separate entities.

For many decades, the building and later its signature dome (said to be modeled after St. Peter's Basilica in Vatican City) stood out in the downtown skyline. Today the brick and stone structure is dwarfed by surrounding commercial and residential towers. It and the Basilica of Saint Louis, King of France (a.k.a., the Old Cathedral), stand as visible reminders of St. Louis as it once was. These properties, along with the Gateway Arch and its recently redesigned surrounding property, comprise Gateway Arch National Park.

Most significant of the countless historic moments at the courthouse were the trials of Dred Scott and his wife, Harriet, who sued for freedom from enslavement in 1847 and 1850. A decision was eventually handed down by the U.S. Supreme Court. These actions helped people form strong opinions about slavery in the United States, ultimately leading to the Civil War.

The Old Courthouse is listed in the National Park Service's National Underground Railroad Network to Freedom. It is open for tours that include its beautifully painted dome ceiling and restored courtrooms.

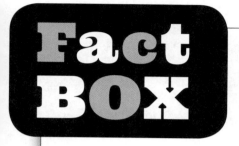

**Fact BOX**

If you visit the Old Courthouse, check out part of the iron fence outside. No, your eyes aren't playing tricks on you. Part of the fence includes a wrought iron turtle motif. The courthouse was abandoned in 1930 when the new Civil Courts Building opened. The National Park Service took over maintenance of the old building when it was determined to be historically significant. The ornamental turtle fence was built a few years later as part of restoration work by local company Kupferer Bros. Ornamental Iron Works Inc. According to an on-site National Park Service ranger, few written details about the fence exist. But according to oral tradition, the fence was built to honor a longtime maintenance worker and his pet turtle. In the late 1800s, sexton James Quigley was described as "the keeper of the courthouse" for the city of St. Louis, a job he held for twenty to thirty years. During the 1870s, Quigley lovingly cared for a resident turtle that hung out in a nearby fountain. A local newspaper printed an obituary for the turtle after it froze to death one winter. Quigley supposedly said, "That turtle was the only thing in the Courthouse that didn't cost the taxpayers money!" And FYI, Kupferer Brothers Iron Works is still in business in Crestwood. Gotta love longtime locals.

# What's the story behind the Eads Bridge?

## A bridge ahead of its time

Talk about a modern marvel. St. Louis's Eads Bridge, dedicated on July 4, 1874, was that and then some. The bridge was the first large triple-span bridge and the first railroad bridge to cross the mighty Mississippi River at St. Louis. It was the first bridge to use entirely cantilevered construction for its superstructure and the first to use tubular cord to frame the bridge's steel arches. Plus its limestone support piers were sunk to an incredible depth of more than one hundred feet beneath the churning surface of the Mississippi and into bedrock by using a French process called pneumatic caissons. The caissons allowed workers to build the piers underwater while they occupied airtight chambers filled with compressed air.

And if that wasn't enough, it was designed by a self-educated engineer who had no experience building bridges— successful St. Louis businessman James Buchanan Eads. Eads also wanted to use a fairly new material, structural steel

 **TREASURES**

alloy, rather than iron in his proposed arch bridge. His critics said he was proposing the impossible. Eads, however, believed in himself and his plans. He replied, "Must we admit that, because a thing has never been done, it never can be?"

In other words, a lot could have gone wrong during the seven years it took to build the magnificent bridge, but it didn't. Although the Eads Bridge doesn't have the wow factor of the more recently constructed Stan Musial Veterans Memorial Bridge, it continues its usefulness. And it was named a National Historic Landmark in 1964 and a National Historic Civil Engineering Landmark in 1971. Other bridges have come and gone, but the artistic Eads Bridge remains.

The last train crossed the Eads Bridge in 1974. In 1993, MetroLink refurbished the bridge's lower deck and began using it for St. Louis's light-rail system.

## Fact BOX

If you've ever participated in deep-water scuba diving and have risen to the water surface too quickly, chances are you may have experienced the bends. The bends are extremely painful stomach cramps, and along with joint pains, headaches, and sometimes temporary paralysis, were experienced by many Eads Bridge workers after toiling in the depths of the Mississippi River in pressurized airtight containers. Visitors who went below the water surface to check the project's progress also were afflicted with this decompression malady. Some people experienced extreme discomfort; others did not. By the time the bridge was completed, more than a dozen men had died following time spent underwater.

# St. Louis's French Connection Continues Today.

Look around St. Louis. French heritage connections are everywhere.

For example, that three-pronged, flower-looking thing that resembles a Boy Scout symbol is called the fleur-de-lis (French for "flower of the lily"). It graces everything from street signs and company logos to St. Louis's city flag. So what is it and why is it displayed so frequently?

Traditional use of the symbol dates back centuries to represent French royalty. It later was used to symbolize French land claims and for decorative purposes. Many St. Louisans are proud of their French heritage, thus the popularity of the fleur-de-lis.

But you won't find the fleur-de-lis on display in the Archdiocese of St. Louis, the overseeing organization of the Catholic Church in St. Louis and ten nearby counties. "While the fleur-de-lis is not an official Catholic symbol, we definitely know what it means," says archdiocese spokesperson Gabe Jones. "The lily represents the Virgin Mary. The flower's three petals symbolize the Holy Trinity— Father, Son, Holy Spirit."

So it's a multipronged symbol used to represent political, artistic, dynastic, scholastic, and sometimes religious enterprises in St. Louis.

Gotta love a multitasker, right?

 **HISTORIC INFLUENCES**

And then there's that St. Louis issue with incorrectly pronounced French street names.

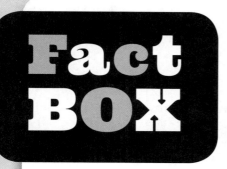

St. Louis's founders were French fur traders. The French names they gave to early streets were changed to English in 1809. Time passed and the village grew. Some additional streets were named for the early French pioneers.

There are two schools of thought about French street name mispronunciations: Some speculate that people of French descent carried a years-long grudge after the French Revolution and that they intentionally mispronounced French words as an act of rebellion. Others surmise that immigrants settling here from countries like Germany didn't know how to correctly pronounce French names. Mispronunciations became part of the city's legendary vernacular.

## Fact BOX

And there's yet another French connection. St. Louis's iconic City Hall building with its two distinct stone colors (pink-orange Roman brick and Missouri pink granite) plus buff-color sandstone is based on the Paris, France, city hall building, Hotel de Ville.

A design competition was authorized in 1889. The French Renaissance Revival building design of George Richard Mann from St. Joseph was selected. Construction began in July 1890, but was not completed until November 1904. The building features towers and dormer windows, plus it recalls architectural elements of the Chateau de Chambord in France's Loire Valley. Plus it has an ornate rotunda, various balconies, lots of marble surfaces, and looks pretty impressive from the street!

A little-known secret is that some of the building's exterior details were never completed. Each side of the building features ornamental dormers called belvederes. The belvederes have blank limestone spaces that originally were designed to feature carved ornamentation. Was this deviation from the plans due to an oversight or a lack of funds? Guess we'll never know.

# What role did St. Louis play in the civil rights movement?

## Equality for all

The road to secure civil rights has been lengthy. St. Louis has witnessed significant civil rights events, including the following:

Struggles began in 1819, before statehood. The country's first civil rights demonstration happened at the Old Courthouse, protesting Missouri's admission as a slave state.

Pastor John Berry Meachum and his wife, Mary, were slaves. John worked for their freedom. Missouri law banned educating blacks, but in the 1820s the Meachums created Missouri's first church for blacks. They circumvented the law with the Floating Freedom School on the Mississippi River, where blacks could learn literacy. They also participated in Underground Railroad activities.

In 1847, Dred and Harriet Scott sued for their freedom in St. Louis.

Sumner High School opened in 1875 as the first black high school west of the Mississippi River.

Saint Louis University first admitted black students in 1944. It was the state's first all-Caucasian university to do so. In the same

## HISTORIC INFLUENCES

year, lunch counter sit-ins were held, challenging whites-only serving policies.

Racially restrictive housing covenants were commonplace here until J. D. and Ethel Shelley's 1945 home purchase in a restricted area. This was challenged by neighbors and went to the U.S. Supreme Court. The Shelleys won.

In 1963, minority leaders targeted Jefferson Bank's discriminatory hiring policies. Hundreds peacefully protested outside the bank in "acts of civil disobedience." Some were jailed. The result was changed hiring policies. Other area companies followed.

In 2014, the Black Lives Matter movement was established here.

FREEDOM OF RESIDENCE

MEANS

YOUR RIGHT TO AN INTEGRATED NEIGHBORHOOD

LET US TELL YOU WHERE

## Fact Box

The Rev. Dr. Martin Luther King Jr. made at least six public visits to St. Louis. His first visit was to Kiel Auditorium in April 1957.

Dr. King spoke to approximately 2,500 people at the United Hebrew Temple in November 1960, receiving a fifteen-minute standing ovation. He spoke at Washington Tabernacle Baptist Church in May 1963.

In September 1963, he returned to St. Louis and spoke to more than three thousand at Temple Israel. This was a few weeks after his "I Have a Dream" speech at the March on Washington for Jobs and Freedom. He spoke at Christ Church Cathedral in March 1964.

Dr. King also spoke to a student government organization at Saint Louis University in 1964. Included was this quote: "While the law can't change the hearts of men, it does change the habits. And, in time, habits change attitudes."

# The Civil War

- **Missouri was a border state during the Civil War.**

- **Were St. Louisans Union or Confederate?**

- **Why were German immigrants so important to the Union army in St. Louis during the Civil War?**

- **Did the Underground Railroad operate in St. Louis?**

## Important considerations

Missouri was impacted by the slavery issue leading to the Civil War. Social injustice, discrimination, and prejudice were aspects of European society that led thousands of Germans to flee for the democracy of America. During the 1840s–50s, boatloads of Germans arrived on U.S. shores. Many settled in St. Louis and rural western Missouri. By the 1850s, a high percentage of St. Louisans were of German descent.

Germans related to the plight of slaves in the United States Many settling here were outspoken thinkers who formed a tight-knit community. By 1861, some wanted neutrality regarding slavery, but others chose sides. Rifts developed. Volunteer

## HISTORIC INFLUENCES

regiments were organized by both sides. Riots happened, with the city's arsenal in jeopardy. People died.

Missouri governor Claiborne Jackson favored secession from the Union. However, the German-born opposition was strong enough that a majority vote to leave never passed.

"If it hadn't been for the huge influx of German immigrants to Missouri beginning in the 1830s, slave-owning residents likely would have seceded and supported the Confederacy," says Dorris Keeven-Franke, executive director of the Missouri Germans Consortium. "It was necessary for the German population to join the Union army and become involved. Germans like Friedrich Muench and Arnold Krekel were abolitionists who filled Missouri's German newspapers with their writings and led the efforts for Missouri's emancipation proclamation. Many historians believe that if not for the Germans, the outcome could have been different."

Keeven-Franke says Germans were instrumental in the formation of the U.S. Colored Troops. "Quite often Germans were the only ones willing to serve as their regimental leaders. The Germans held recruiting sign-ups despite opposition. These regiments were not even named for Missouri despite being formed here. These units later created educational opportunities like Lincoln University after the war."

# "Where'd you go to high school?" and other St. Louis questions

## How St. Louisans categorize each other

 **UNIQUELY ST. LOUIS**

Meet a lifelong St. Louis resident for the first time and you're likely to hear this question: "Where'd you go to high school?"

Doesn't matter how old you are or what part of town you live in now, the question will be asked. So why do St. Louisans ask this question, and why do they care?

"I haven't found a good reason for this question," says *St. Louis Post-Dispatch* columnist and longtime St. Louis resident Joe Holleman. "Is it a class judgment question? Maybe. More likely it has to do with the number of schools, particularly parochial schools, in the St. Louis area.

"At one time there was a higher percentage of kids attending Catholic schools in St. Louis than in any other place in the country. Perhaps the question began years ago as a way to identify if someone was Catholic or not."

So is this question asked in other large cities? "I've not found it in other cities," Holleman says. "I don't think people in other cities focus on the high school question."

Other questions asked by longtime St. Louis residents include:

## "Do you live in the city or the county?"
## "What part of the county do you live in?"
## "What side of the river (insert Mississippi or Missouri) do you live on?"

So why all the questions? Socioeconomic determiners? Status indicators? Stereotyping mechanisms? Personal curiosity? Perhaps all of the above.

# I see it's a garage sale, but where's the garage?

## The unspoken rules of St. Louis garage sales

St. Louisans love a good garage sale. In St. Louis, garage sale is a generic term used to describe for-sale items displayed not only in garages, but also in driveways, yards, basements, the back of pickup trucks, on sidewalks, and in carports.

Household items, toys, books, clothing, furniture, exercise equipment, athletic equipment, baby items, sports memorabilia, and more. If you're looking for it or collecting it, drive around long enough on a Wednesday or Saturday and you're likely to find it. The earlier in the morning you hit the road, the more likely you are to find treasures.

Joe Holleman, *St. Louis Post-Dispatch* columnist and expert on all things St. Louis, says he's wondered why garage sales are held only on Wednesdays and Saturdays. "I think it goes back to the days before electronic media, when newspapers carried pages of classified ads and offered discounted advertising rates if you ran an ad on a Wednesday or Saturday."

 **UNIQUELY ST. LOUIS**

# Fact BOX

St. Louis garage sales have a few unspoken rules that you'll only hear from seasoned pickers. These include targeting certain neighborhoods (some have the reputation for offering higher-quality items), cruising these areas well before the standard start time (7 a.m.), taking an ample supply of cash, and bartering for lower prices whenever possible. Also, it's not cool to approach a bathrobe-clad resident strolling to grab the newspaper— even if you can clearly see a sale is about to happen there. If it's not 7 a.m., don't ask for a quick sneak peek.

FYI, according to the St. Louis City Revised Code, Chapter 15.156, Division IX, Miscellaneous Offenses and Regulations: "It shall be unlawful to conduct any sale at retail in the front yard of any residentially zoned property, as the term 'front yard' is herein defined, which said sale is known as a yard sale, garage sale or lawn sale." The penalty for violation (if you're caught) is a fine of "not less than $50.00 nor more than $500.00 or imprisonment for not more than 90 days or both such fine and imprisonment."

# Why was St. Louis called the Mound City? Do they like candy bars that much?

## Ancient civilizations dug St. Louis.

The landscape of today's St. Louis looks much different than it did when Frenchmen Pierre Laclede and August Chouteau settled here in the 1700s. At that time, the land was dotted with several dozen enormous mounds thought to have been created by ancient civilizations.

The close proximity to the Mississippi, Missouri, and Illinois Rivers, plus fertile land, made the area an appealing place to settle. Some guessed the mounds were mass burial sites. Others said they had ceremonial significance and contained relics from daily life.

The mounds became landmarks. River travelers knew they were near St. Louis when they spotted the mounds in the distance. St. Louis acquired the nickname Mound City.

As the city grew during the nineteenth century, the mounds were leveled and built over. Dirt from the mounds was used in the production of bricks and as fill during railroad construction. More than a dozen mounds in Forest Park were destroyed in preparation for the 1904 World's Fair.

Today only one large mound remains in St. Louis. Sugarloaf Mound, located south of downtown on a bluff overlooking the Mississippi River, most likely survived thanks to a house built on its peak decades ago. The mound was listed on the National Register of Historic Places in 1984. The Osage Nation now owns the property and plans to preserve it as a sacred site.

Several area businesses include Mound City in their names, but the reference is to the earthen mounds once found here, not candy.

# Why is that guy Ted Drewes so popular? Is he giving away bags of money?

## Frozen custard's popularity in The Lou

Say the name "Ted Drewes" to any St. Louisan and you'll likely see a big grin. Ted is just that well known. Generations of St. Louis families have grown up enjoying Ted's sweet, creamy frozen custard. It's like a rite of passage.

Drive down Chippewa Street (one of two locations) on a warm evening and you're likely to witness the Ted Drewes phenomenon—long lines, slow traffic, street-party atmosphere. Most customers stop for a frozen custard concoction called a concrete. (FYI, the consistency is so thick that servers prove it by turning it upside down before handing it to customers—and the contents stay put.)

It all started with Ted Drewes Sr. He didn't invent frozen custard, but he introduced it to St. Louis in 1930. The automobile

 **UNIQUELY ST. LOUIS**

industry was young and quickly becoming mobile. Ted set up stands in several St. Louis locations before opening one along what became U.S. Route 66 (today's Chippewa Street)—the Mother Road. And so began a St. Louis tradition.

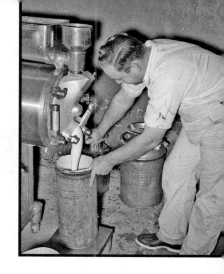

Ted Jr. runs the business started by his father. "It really is good, guys and . . . gals!" he says. But he isn't the only frozen custard vendor in town. Others include Fritz's, Andy's, and Mr. Wizard's. Customers say the custard taste varies according to each establishment's unique recipe (some say honey is the secret ingredient).

Another thing you'll find at Ted Drewes and the other frozen custard stands is socialization—the chance to mix and mingle with friends, neighbors, pets, and even strangers. It's a tradition St. Louisans embrace.

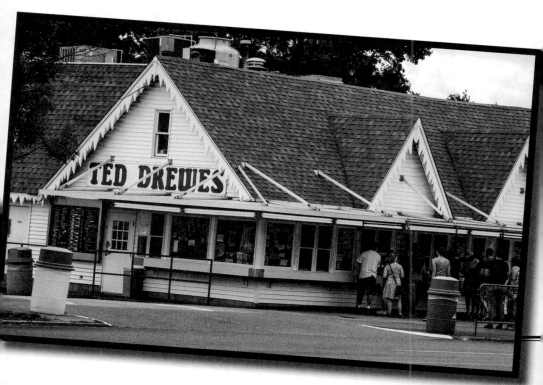

# What sayeth the Veiled Prophet? And doeth we care?

## St. Louis and its storied traditions

Maybe it was a quaint fairy tale. Or maybe it wasn't.

Throughout its history, St. Louis has been a city of distinct socioeconomic classes with racial and gender disparities. An elite group of people ran the city.

Uprisings by working-class St. Louisans in the 1870s were a cause of concern to the city fathers. In response, those in positions of social and political authority devised a secret society that in 1878 hosted what became an annual fable-like pageant and parade to entertain the masses and at the same time send a message.

The message was that the elite control the city and will continue to do so even if armed action is necessary. The message was conveyed in the persona of the Veiled Prophet from the Kingdom of Khorassan, a.k.a. the Grand Oracle. His head

 **UNIQUELY ST. LOUIS**

covering and clothing resembled that of Klansmen. He was accompanied by costumed assistants bearing weapons.

In addition, each year a Queen of Love and Beauty (a daughter of one of the VP members) was selected by the organization to "rule" over a ball (debutante gathering).

Many St. Louisans were enthralled by the lavish show of wealth parading through the city streets each year. They embraced the mythical story and attended VP events by the tens of thousands. Others saw it as a flaunting of elitist wealth.

"The organization, through the parade and ball it sponsored, made the members feel like good fathers both to the city and to their own daughters," says Dr. Thomas M. Spencer, director of honors student affairs at Eastern Illinois University and author of *The St. Louis Veiled Prophet Celebration—Power on Parade, 1877–1995*. "The increased trade during the St. Louis Fair helped the city, thus making these men feel they were being good city fathers. The success of the Veiled Prophet ball in giving their daughters a 'night to remember,' as well as helping the daughters find good marriage prospects, made them feel they were being good fathers in the usual sense."

Television brought increased attention to the VP festivities, but the mid-twentieth century's growing civil rights movement brought about a steep decline in their popularity. In recent years the Veiled Prophet organization has become more diverse and inclusive. It has adopted a more community-minded philosophy and assists with the city's Independence Day celebration.

# Here's to your health!

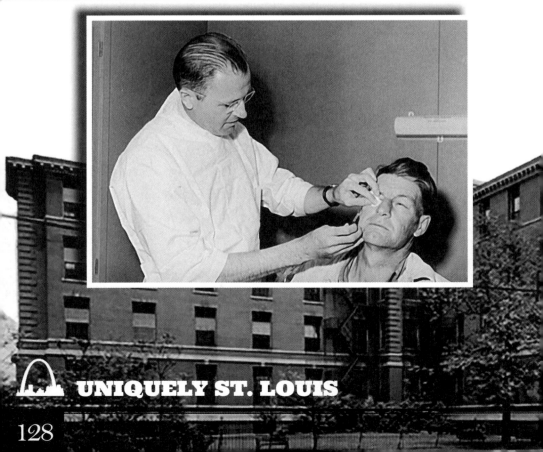

**UNIQUELY ST. LOUIS**

Big cities have strengths and weaknesses. Something St. Louis does, and does really well, is health care.

Washington University and Saint Louis University have renowned medical schools and multiple hospital affiliations. Barnes-Jewish College of Nursing traces its roots to 1905.

SSM Health is headquartered in St. Louis and is one of the largest Catholic healthcare systems in the United States. It has affiliate operations in four states.

BJC Health Systems has a lengthy history dating to the 1890s and includes the combined resources and expertise of what once were three separate hospital systems—Barnes Hospital, Jewish Hospital, and Christian Health Services. Numerous medical "firsts" have happened at these hospitals, including the use of gloves in operating rooms, the installation of an electronic data processing system in a hospital, and nerve transplants. St. Louis medical professionals also have been leaders in laparoscopic surgery and in vitro fertilization.

St. Louis Children's Hospital dates to 1879. It was the first children's hospital west of the Mississippi River and was founded by eight women. The hospital provides pediatric services to children from around the world. Among its specialties are the treatment of cerebral palsy, cleft palate, and epilepsy, and bone marrow and liver transplants.

# Was St. Louis really *first* in shoes?

## Walk a mile (or more) in our shoes.

"St. Louis: first in booze, first in shoes, and last in the American League" was a twentieth-century slogan referencing the numerous breweries and footwear companies located here. At that time, the American League's St. Louis Browns called St. Louis home. The Browns' performance was less than stellar, and the team was eventually sold. But for decades, St. Louis maintained its position as an important brewing city (due to the German population influence) and a major footwear hub (dozens of headquarters and production facilities called St. Louis home).

St. Louis's location and proximity to resources led to it becoming a shoe industry hub. Founded in 1764 as a fur-trading village, fur and leather sources remained plentiful throughout the ninteenth century. By 1900, St. Louis was one of the largest cities in population and industrial development. The 1904 World's Fair promised to bring worldwide attention to the city.

The city's location near rivers, railroads, and the middle of the United States made it a transportation crossroads. It attracted people migrating west from East Coast cities. It also attracted business. But geography and transportation weren't the only factors

## UNIQUELY ST. LOUIS

William Howard Taft, a big man with wide feet, was president in 1909. He couldn't find comfortable shoes. He sent a letter to "my dear sirs" at Brown Shoe asking for custom-made shoes, noting his doctor could provide precise foot measurements. The company agreed, producing a patent leather blucher, "Taft special D width." Brown Shoe publicized the letter and its famous customer.

Shoes were interchangeable until the early nineteenth century. Rights and lefts didn't exist.

"Made in the USA" has been important to consumers since the late eighteenth century. At that time, France and England shipped quantities of footwear to the United States, causing sales of locally made shoes to decline. To encourage local production, Congress placed tariffs on foreign-produced footwear.

contributing to the growth. Innovation and hard work helped St. Louis become a leader in footwear.

Entrepreneurs like George Warren Brown and A. D. Brown saw St. Louis's location as an asset for getting leather supplies and manpower to run factories, plus it had easy access to transportation. Others soon followed the Brown brothers' lead and established footwear enterprises. Washington Avenue and nearby buzzed with activity. Companies manufactured and shipped thousands of pairs of footwear each day from Shoe City, USA. Brands like Buster Brown, Naturalizer, and Red Goose were born here.

St. Louis remained a footwear leader until the 1960s. U.S. production costs increased, and companies outsourced production to cheap-labor countries. Jobs were eliminated and factories closed.

George Warren Brown's innovative company, now known as Caleres, still has its headquarters here. Other footwear companies also call St. Louis home.

# Who is this

## character and should I avoid him?

### Never too old to rock and roll

This Sweetmeat guy really gets around town. His porcine visage sports headphones, round black shades, and a nose ring. Hanging from his mouth is something that resembles an item legally available in Colorado. In a word, he has attitude.

Through the years, Sweetmeat's been shown full length, rocking black skinny jeans and holding a guitar. He's been featured in print advertisements and on countless billboards, T-shirts, bumper stickers, and a host of other promotional paraphernalia, including a giant inflatable. Exactly who is this popular hip porker whose face is recognizable throughout the world? Sweetmeat is the beloved symbol and mascot of the oldest continuously operating rock and roll station in the country—FM radio station KSHE 95.

KSHE has been playing the very best real rock music (not pop) since 1967. Sweetmeat began representing the station in the early 1970s. The album cover of an obscure Canadian blues band named Blodwyn Pig caught the eye of station owner Shelley

Grafman. One thing led to another, and the album's pig image was introduced as KSHE's new logo.

According to veteran broadcaster and former KSHE disc jockey Ron Stevens, the station sponsored a pig-naming contest in 1974. An Affton teen suggested the name Sweetmeat. His prize for providing the winning name? A whopping fifty pounds of bacon. "I always wondered what a kid did with that much bacon," says Stevens.

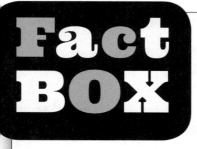

Once upon a time, a small radio station was born in the basement of a St. Louis area home (Crestwood). Its musical format included orchestra instrumentals and polkas—popular choices for early 1960s listeners. The station's target market was women and homemakers. The station's call letters, KSHE, provided a convenient tie-in with its target audience.

But the station never became a commercial success. In 1964, the station was sold to two Chicago entrepreneurs. The music format was about to change, and history was about to be made. Fast-forward 50 years. Generations of KSHE listeners have grown up to the sounds of musical groups ranging from Led Zeppelin, Rush, AC/DC, and Sammy Hagar to local favorites like Mama's Pride and Head East. From kite-flies and "the window" at the early station to the Real Rock Army, 80+-year-old DJ Ruth Hutchinson, and countless concerts, KSHE, the home of "real rock radio," has provided the musical soundtrack for thousands of St. Louis listeners through the years.

KSHE's first rock DJs were in their late teens and had no broadcast experience. Veteran broadcaster and media professional Ron Stevens was the oldest of the DJ crew when he began work at KSHE. He was 21. "We played the music we wanted to hear and we had a good time," he says. In 2017, Stevens released a documentary film detailing the station's history, *Never Say Goodbye: The KSHE Documentary*.

# What's the only Vatican-verified miracle to have occurred in the Midwest?

## It's a miracle!

A church called the Shrine of St. Joseph (St. Joseph Catholic Church) sits near downtown. The Archdiocese of St. Louis says it's the site of the only Vatican-authenticated miracle to occur in the Midwest.

Jesuits founded the church in the 1840s in what was a German neighborhood. The parish grew and added a school. By the 1860s, the church held five capacity Sunday services in a sanctuary holding 1,200 people.

German immigrant Ignatius Strecker lived nearby with his wife and children. He worked at a soap factory. In 1861, he was injured at work when a piece of iron hit him in the chest. There was no wound, but he was in severe pain. His condition worsened and he couldn't work.

A doctor opened him and found deteriorating bones. Other doctors treated respiratory problems, but nothing more could be done.

 **UNIQUELY ST. LOUIS**

In March 1864, Jesuit priest Francis Xavier Weninger visited St. Joseph, preaching about seventeenth-century priest Peter Claver. Claver supposedly had intercessory prayer power. Weninger had a Claver bone fragment called a first-class relic.

Strecker got to church, venerated the relic, and suddenly felt better. He returned to work and lived another fifteen years.

Many believed Strecker was healed through intercession by Peter Claver via the relic. Following a canonical investigation, Rome declared the miracle authentic.

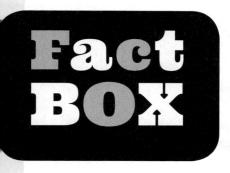

**Fact BOX**

By the 1960s, the neighborhood was declining. The church was crumbling, caked with pigeon droppings and spray-painted graffiti. Once ornate statues were broken.

A group distressed about the church's condition took action. Called the Shrine of St. Joseph Friends, they established a not-for-profit to make repairs. Supplies were donated. Fund-raisers were held. The goal was to restore the sanctuary (sometimes referred to as the Altar of Answered Prayers) exactly as constructed, including original paint and finishes. Toothbrushes were used to remove grime. Tons of droppings were removed from the bell towers.

Two decades and millions of dollars later, the Shrine of St. Joseph and the organ are restored. Both are on the National Register of Historic Places.

Trivia: The shrine houses statues of the Blessed Mother and baby Jesus that were made for Notre Dame Cathedral in Paris, France. Due to long-ago Franco-Prussian political differences, they somehow ended up here.

# Public parks both large and small

St. Louis loves its public parks. They serve as neighborhood anchors, providing needed green space where adults and children can gather for recreation and socialization.

The city of St. Louis has 110 parks encompassing more than three thousand acres. St. Louisans' appreciation of their public spaces dates to the city's early days when French settlers brought the custom of setting aside common fields for community gardens. From these developed the city's parks both large and small.

Forest Park (1,293 acres) was established in 1876 and is one of the nation's largest urban parks. It hosted the 1904 World's Fair and is home to the Saint Louis Zoo, the Saint Louis Art

**URBAN OASES**

Museum, the Missouri History Museum, and the Muny (the oldest and largest outdoor musical theater in the United States).

Dan Skillman, commissioner of parks for the city of St. Louis, names Forest Park as his favorite but finds Lafayette Park one of the city's most interesting. "It has great Victorian features and is one of the only parks with a wrought iron fence around it," he says. "It has hidden features, grotto areas, lakes, and strolling areas."

# Fact BOX

St. Louis's oldest parks (Gravois, Laclede, and Mount Pleasant) date to 1812. The newest, Chouteau Park and Taylor Park, opened in 2007 and 2008. From the large and lavishly landscaped (Forest Park and Tower Grove) to half-acre Minnesota and Hill Park, each is unique. The Parks and Forestry Departments employ 200 full-time and 150 seasonal employees, including an arborist.

# Grant's Farm

Head southwest down Gravois Road and you can't miss it. It's the long stretch of undeveloped bucolic green space on the right. And no, your eyes aren't deceiving you. Those are indeed American bison, antelope, and zebra grazing contentedly as traffic zooms by. Welcome to Grant's Farm, St. Louis's other animal kingdom.

Grant's Farm once belonged to President and Mrs. Ulysses S. Grant (the couple's rustic cabin remains on the property). In 1903, Adolphus Busch of Anheuser-Busch fame built a sprawling German-style country home and barn for his son, August A. Busch Sr.

Time passed. Soon a menagerie of animals representing more than a hundred species from around the world became Grant's Farm residents along with Busch family members. Beginning in 1954, August A. "Gussie" Busch Jr. opened parts of the farm to tourists and guests. Then, as now, admission is free.

Grant's Farm is open to the public from spring until fall. It attracts more than six hundred thousand visitors annually.

**URBAN OASES**

# Fact BOX

Budweiser Clydesdales, the large draught horses long identified with Anheuser-Busch products, live and are bred on the grounds of Grant's Farm. They were first used by A-B in 1933 to celebrate the repeal of Prohibition. August A. Busch Jr. remembered draft horses that once pulled beer wagons in Germany. He purchased a team of six horses to pull a custom A-B wagon down Pennsylvania Avenue to deliver a case of Budweiser to President Franklin D. Roosevelt. The promotion was an instant success, assuring the Clydesdales' permanent association with the brewery.

Approximately fifty Clydesdales enjoy the lavish facilities at Grant's Farm. St. Louis is home to three traveling A-B Clydesdale hitch teams. Each consists of ten horses that travel to promote A-B products. Hitch teams are rotated between the farm and the on-site stable at the downtown brewery.

About forty Clydesdales are born each year, but not all make a hitch team. According to a Grant's Farm tour representative, a horse needs the following characteristics to qualify for a team: four white stocking feet, a white forehead blaze, black mane and tail, and a dark brown coat. Clydesdales that qualify begin training with older horses at about age three. They can begin traveling at about age four. Approximately one hundred Clydesdales that are not part of hitch teams reside at nearby Warm Springs Ranch.

The Clydesdales have a daily routine. Each horse's signature hooves are washed every day. They get a full body wash each Friday. Each is walked by hand for about an hour. Horses are rotated from the brewery to Grant's Farm so they can run and get additional exercise.

The Clydesdales live in climate-controlled facilities. Each daily consumes one to twelve pounds of mixed feed, thirty-five to forty pounds of hay, and as much as thirty gallons of water. A Clydesdale's life span is approximately twenty years. What a life!

139

# I see dead people.
## With cool headstones.

**Bellefontaine and Calvary Cemeteries— where the in-crowd spends eternity**

No matter life's successes, everybody dies. And where but cemeteries do the famous and nameless come together?

St. Louis was the gateway to the west in 1849. With a nod to its French founders, it followed a Parisian trend, the rural cemetery movement, establishing cities of the dead far from downtown. The first was Bellefontaine Cemetery, an artistically designed 314-acre parcel located northwest of town.

In 1854, Calvary Cemetery was established when the Roman Catholic Archdiocese of St. Louis purchased 470 acres alongside Bellefontaine Cemetery. Then, as now, St. Louisans liked to do

**URBAN OASES**

things in a *big* way. "We became among the largest cemetery providers in the state," says Calvary Cemetery counselor Matt DeWitt. "You can actually see the history of St. Louis unfold here."

Elaborate stone mausoleums, statues, and markers stand as perpetual monuments to the thousands buried in both cemeteries. And Bellefontaine, also an arboretum, shares its beauty with the living, hosting weddings, runs, and tours. "Visitors can connect names with family history as well as city and U.S. history," says Richard Lay, vice president of Bellefontaine's cemetery association.

With more than eighty-seven thousand gravesites, Bellefontaine is less than half full. Calvary, too, has plenty of room for more.

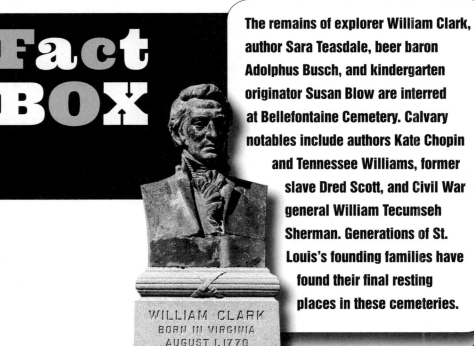

# Fact BOX

The remains of explorer William Clark, author Sara Teasdale, beer baron Adolphus Busch, and kindergarten originator Susan Blow are interred at Bellefontaine Cemetery. Calvary notables include authors Kate Chopin and Tennessee Williams, former slave Dred Scott, and Civil War general William Tecumseh Sherman. Generations of St. Louis's founding families have found their final resting places in these cemeteries.

WILLIAM CLARK
BORN IN VIRGINIA
AUGUST 1, 1770
ENTERED INTO LIFE ETERNAL
SEPTEMBER 1, 1838
SOLDIER, EXPLORER,
STATESMAN AND PATRIOT
HIS LIFE IS WRITTEN
IN THE HISTORY OF HIS COUNTRY.

# Why does the Missouri Botanical Garden contain a Japanese garden?

## A pocket of serene beauty

An Asian oasis exists in St. Louis. The Japanese Garden (Seiwa-en) is a relative newcomer to the Missouri Botanical Garden. From 1904 to 1972, the fourteen-acre site it now occupies was called the North American tract and was filled with trees.

Members of the Japanese American Citizens League (JACL) wanted to install a Japanese garden there. An agreement was reached, and the JACL hired famed architect and garden designer Koichi Kawana to make it a reality.

"The placement of everything is significant, including each rock and the use of odd-numbered objects," says Missouri Botanical Garden archivist Andrew Colligan. "It's typical of traditional Japanese gardens with 'hide and reveal' vantage points. One must go around corners to discover the next visual-interest items."

**URBAN OASES**

The garden features plants, a lake, waterfalls, traditional bridges, lanterns and islands, peonies, and more than four hundred rhododendron and azalea specimens. Also included is a traditional teahouse fabricated in Japan, a gift of Nagano, Japan, Missouri's sister state. Workers were brought from Japan to assemble the house, which includes no nails. It is located on an island and is closed to the public except for a kick-off tea held at the start of the annual Labor Day weekend Japanese Festival. The first festival was held in 1976. It's one of the oldest and largest festivals of its kind in the United States.

"It's a garden designed for all four seasons," says Colligan. "It looks attractive and beautiful in the summer as well as with snowfall during the winter."

# Fact BOX

The Missouri Botanical Garden is forever growing, changing, and evolving. Renovation work recently was completed on founder Henry Shaw's circa-1859 library and herbarium. The building had been closed to the public since 1982. During renovations, portraits of three well-known botanists were uncovered. Portraits of Carl Linnaeus, who developed a system of naming and classifying organisms, and botanist George Engelmann, who identified plants of the American West, were restored. Shaw named the garden's Linnean House as a tribute to Linnaeus. Engelmann was Shaw's mentor. The renovated building reopened as the Stephen and Peter Sachs Museum Building.

# Is Cardinals Nation a religious group?

## Almost. St. Louis has baseball fever.

The arrival of spring means one thing to St. Louis Cardinals fans —the start of Major League Baseball.

Some people call Cardinals fanaticism Redbird fever. Others refer to the thousands of loyal baseball Cardinals fans as Cardinals Nation. Whatever they're called, fans of the National League's St. Louis Cardinals welcome spring and opening day at Busch Stadium with frenzied enthusiasm.

Cardinals Nation is also the name of a venue at Ballpark Village, a sports-centered entertainment area where loyal fans gather to support the Redbirds on game days and throughout the year. Today's Busch Stadium is the team's third home.

**SPORTS**

It encompasses twenty-eight acres (a whopping 1,270,000 square feet), including Ballpark Village and seating for approximately 45,000 fans.

Attending a game at Busch Stadium is an experience like no other. The sights and sounds, as well as the tastes and smells, have entertained generations of Redbird fans. And postseason playoff games are memories in the making for St. Louis baseball fanatics.

**Fact BOX**

Established in 1882, the St. Louis Cardinals have a colorful history. Some of baseball's greatest players have worn Redbird jerseys, including Stan Musial, Dizzy Dean, Lou Brock, Ozzie Smith, and Bob Gibson. The Cardinals' Branch Rickey is credited with developing baseball's farm club system. The Cardinals have won eleven World Series championships and nineteen National League pennants, making them one of baseball's most successful teams.

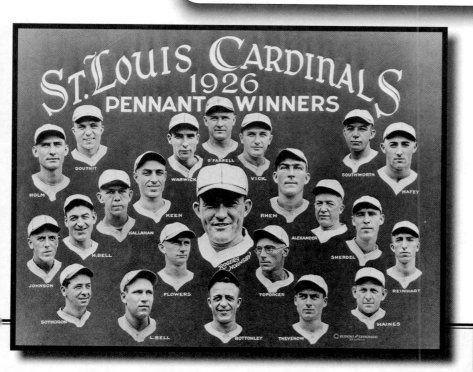

# The St. Louis Blues are more than just a hockey team.

## St. Louis and its Blue Note fans

**SPORTS**

Anyone who's attended a St. Louis Blues hockey game knows it's a memorable experience. Blues fans are faithful and dedicated followers of the Note. While the the team has never won the Stanley Cup (the National Hockey League's championship trophy), its loyal fans have flocked to arenas to cheer on "the boys" since the team first came to town in 1967.

"I think the key to the St. Louis Blues' huge following is the fact that the ownership is local," says a source with the St. Louis Blues Hockey Club. "The owners appreciate the fans and the pride St. Louis has in the team." Home hockey games draw eighteen to nineteen thousand fans, with tickets for weekend games often in short supply. Frequent promotional giveaway nights enable fans to collect one-of-a-kind souvenirs and collectibles.

"It's been interesting to see how the game of hockey has evolved in the last fifty years here," says the Blues source. "Today the players focus on strength training and safety. In the past, players didn't wear masks and helmets."

Fact
BOX

St. Louis Blues hockey games are played at Enterprise Center, the team's home since 1995. Home games include regular features like appearances by Louie, the team's mascot; the smooth moves of Zamboni machines between periods; Towel Man (a longtime fan who tosses a towel when the team scores); a musical power play ditty complete with hand motions; and repetition of the team's mantra, "Let's Go Blues!" The games are fast paced and not for the faint of heart. Opposing players sometimes fight and blood hits the ice.

# Gone but not forgotten

## St. Louis's lost sports franchises

Blame it on owner greed, a lack of public interest, or some of both. Whatever the reason, St. Louis has been home to several professional sports teams—at least for a time. These include the St. Louis Hawks and the Spirits of St. Louis, both basketball teams, and two football teams, the St. Louis Cardinals and the St. Louis Rams.

Oh, and there were the years when St. Louis was home to two baseball teams—the St. Louis Browns (American League) and the St. Louis Cardinals (National League). In 1944, both teams battled it out to become baseball's World Series champions. Not to brag, but that was one of eleven times the Cardinals won the World Series.

The St. Louis Hawks played at Kiel Auditorium from 1955 to 1968.

St. Louis Browns, 1944

**SPORTS**

The team made it to the
National Basketball Association
finals four times (1957, 1958,
1960, 1961), winning the NBA
championship in 1958.

The Spirits of St. Louis
were part of the short-lived
American Basketball Association before it merged with the NBA.
The Spirits played at the old St. Louis Arena (a.k.a. "the Old Barn")
from 1974 to 1976.

The St. Louis Cardinals football franchise was a part of St.
Louis from 1960 to 1987. Sometimes called the Cardiac Cardinals,
the team played outdoors at Sportsman's Park/Busch Stadium and
the second Busch Stadium. They never won the Super Bowl. After
the Cardinals left for Phoenix, it took eight years to bring another
National Football League franchise to St. Louis.

The St. Louis Rams arrived in the Gateway City in 1995 amid
much fanfare. After a few outdoor games at the second Busch
Stadium, the team moved into a new domed stadium in the heart
of downtown. The Rams won Super Bowl XXXIV in 1999. They
played their last home game in St. Louis in December 2015 before
relocating to Los Angeles.

# St. Louis Arena

## The Old Barn

If walls could talk, those of Oakland Avenue's old St. Louis Arena could have spoken volumes. It was the scene of countless memorable moments in twentieth-century St. Louis history.

The building that came to be known as the Arena was unique when it opened in late September 1929. Its ceiling was supported by twenty cantilevered steel trusses, not upright posts. Built to house the National Dairy Show and livestock shows, only one such show was held there. The October 1929 stock market crash put an end to those plans, and soon the building was for sale.

Through the years, the large structure hosted sporting events, conventions, horse and rodeo shows, ice shows, circuses, and concerts. Then, in 1967, businessman Sid Salomon and investors brought professional hockey to the Arena. They called the team the St. Louis Blues.

The Blues quickly garnered a fan base with players like Barclay Plager, Garry Unger, Jacques Plante, and Bernie Federko. In the early days, ticket prices ranged from $2.50 to $6.00, which made it an affordable sport for many St. Louisans. Home hockey games took on a party atmosphere.

**SPORTS**

In 1981, the Arena became the Checkerdome when it was purchased by local company Ralston Purina, whose corporate identity included a red and white checkerboard design. By the 1990s, the Arena's days of usefulness were numbered. A larger modern arena was built in the heart of downtown. The Kiel Center, today called Enterprise Center, became the new home of the St. Louis Blues.

But St. Louisans are sentimental. Seats from the Old Barn were removed and sold prior to the building's implosion in 1999. Today the space is occupied by an office building.

# Why are St. Louisans so obsessed with SOCCER?

## Who's got the ball?

Drive by most any St. Louis–area schoolyard, public playground, or athletic field and you'll see them: dozens of people of all ages playing the game of soccer. Some wear matching team jerseys and shin guards. Others look like they spotted a soccer game in progress and decided to join in. From tots to teens and adults, soccer is extremely popular in St. Louis, and has been for generations, but why? Why are St. Louisans so enamored with kicking around a leather ball?

It's a long story, one that traces its origins across the Atlantic Ocean and back to Europe. From its early settlement days in 1764 and continuing today, St. Louis has attracted immigrants from numerous countries worldwide. Large groups of immigrants from England, Scotland, Ireland, and Italy, began arriving in St. Louis after the Civil War, establishing communities and neighborhoods. They brought with them their foods, culture, and leisure-time activities, including soccer.

Soccer is an extremely physical game, and traditionally Irish soccer enthusiasts have played hard and rough. That trend also came to St. Louis. "Many of the new arrivals were Catholics," says veteran Christian Brothers College (CBC) High School coach Terry Michler. "They built communities around their churches and schools and established youth soccer teams that played against one another. There were some big-time rivalries among teams representing various parishes, and this was still going on in the 1950s and 1960s."

## SPORTS

# Fact BOX

The Catholic Youth Council (CYC) of the Archdiocese of St. Louis has coordinated generations of St. Louis youth soccer players. The organization's involvement continues today. "Teams are formed through individual parishes," says Gabe Jones, spokesperson for the Archdiocese of St. Louis. "The CYC oversees play and the teams on the local level. About a hundred parishes participate in CYC soccer programs. In 2017, 1,461 CYC soccer teams existed in the archdiocese for ages kindergarten through adult." CYC sports director Paul Scovill says, "Soccer is excellent for conditioning. It forms teamwork and involves more strategy than most people realize."

-------------------------------------------------------------------------------------

Ask any St. Louis soccer aficionado to name the sport's local memorable moments and they'll probably mention two years – 1950, when a St. Louis team won the World Cup championship in England, and 1972, when Saint Louis University's soccer team won the National Collegiate Athletic Association's Division 1 soccer championship. The years 1950-1979 were considered the heyday of soccer in St. Louis, with Catholic Youth Council teams numbering almost 450.

Michler has enjoyed a lifelong involvement with St. Louis soccer. He played varsity soccer for CBC for three years. After playing soccer for Rockhurst College and the Kansas City Spurs, Michler was hired to coach soccer at CBC. He took over from legendary soccer coach Bob Horgan, and forty-plus years later he's still there. In fact, he is the winningest soccer coach in the United States, with more than 960 wins to his credit and multiple state championships. About thirty of his former players have become professional soccer players.

"St. Louis remains a soccer town," Michler says. "Team participation by both girls and boys is at an all-time high in our area."

# What is bocce?

## A timeless game for all ages

Italian immigrants began arriving in St. Louis in the late 1800s. By the early 1900s, they were settling in a community southwest of downtown today known as the Hill. They brought with them recipes for a variety of amazing foods, a strong work ethic, and a ball game called bocce.

Bocce is played with two teams of four players each and traces its origins back thousands of years. One team has four green balls, the other has four red balls (reflecting the colors of the Italian flag), and there's a small target ball called a pallino. The game is played on a long narrow court (seventy feet long, ten feet wide) and is similar to shuffleboard—sort of.

Many St. Louisans associate bocce with Milo's Tavern and Bocce Garden on the Hill. "We have two courts and three leagues that play Mondays through Thursdays at 7:30, 8:30, and 9:30 p.m.," says Milo's owner Tom Savio. "But we're open year-round. When the temps are mild in the winter, people are there to play."

Savio opened Milo's in 1975 and built bocce courts in 1989. They've been a popular gathering spot for the sport ever since.

**SPORTS**

The courts are available for open play during the day and frequently host fund-raising tournaments for organizations like nearby St. Ambrose Church and Stray Rescue.

The exact date bocce was first played on the Hill is unclear, but Savio remembers a place called Rose's Bar where it was played for decades. He says one thing sets St. Louis apart when it comes to bocce.

"In St. Louis, everybody pronounces the name like bo-chie. That's what I always heard it called. In other parts of the country, it's pronounced like bot-chie. But my favorite pronunciation happened when someone called up and wanted to know what time the Hibachi leagues played!" Gotta love those St. Louis-isms.

As Milo's says, "Bella Bocce." Keep those bocce balls rolling.

The Hill's Marconi Avenue is home to St. Louis's Italia-America Bocce Club, established in 1975. Through hard work, donated time, fund-raisers, and sheer determination, a group of die-hard bocce lovers created an indoor bocce facility. In 2018, this members-only club hosted the U.S. Bocce Championship.

# Livin' just enough for the city . . . which is different from living in the county; or City Mouse, County Mouse.

## St. Louis City and St. Louis County, a unique municipal arrangement

 WHERE WE LIVE

It probably seemed like a good idea at the time, or so the city fathers thought. In 1877, St. Louis became the first city in the United States to enact a home rule city charter. St. Louis City and St. Louis County, which had been one, formally separated. Each established its own government and judicial systems, municipal services, and taxation rates.

City limit boundaries were defined to allow plenty of space for continued growth and expansion in the decades ahead. At least that was the plan. In reality, St. Louis City experienced rapid growth during the 1880s–1890s. Its position as a transportation crossroads attracted industries. Immigrants, particularly from Germany and Italy, flocked here in search of a new life. It wasn't long before the city reached its boundaries. If growth was to continue, and it did, it would be necessary to expand outside the city limits and into St. Louis County. Plus the city could not annex land belonging to the county.

Transportation options and increased popularity of the automobile, coupled with the desire to leave residential crowding and the grit of downtown industries, led thousands to flee to the suburbs of St. Louis County. The result has been population increases in the county and decreases in the city over the last sixty-five years.

# Brick, brick *everywhere;* or St. Louis 3, Big Bad Wolf 0.

The abundance of brick homes and buildings in St. Louis

Drive through St. Louis and its neighborhoods and you'll notice that sturdy brick structures are everywhere. From residences on quiet, tree-lined streets to low-rise buildings and industrial warehouses near the Mississippi River, brick has long been a popular building material here. "In fact, St. Louis was the largest brick producing city in the world by the turn of the nineteenth century," says Andrew Weil, executive director of the Landmarks Association of St. Louis.

"St. Louis has perfect geology for brick production. A geological feature called the 'Cheltenham syncline' underlies a lot of southwest St. Louis. It is defined by large quantities of clays that are suitable for building brick and refractory brick, as well as coal to fire them."

St. Louisans probably began making and using soft, low-fired brick for chimneys and ovens in the late 1700s. By the late 1840s, it probably was the dominant building material, says Weil. "By the second half of the nineteenth century, advances in technology led to mass machine production of highly standardized, very dense, very hard hydraulic-pressed brick that was produced by the millions and shipped all over the country." St. Louis's brick production hit its peak in the early twentieth century, but St. Louis–produced brick is still in demand.

"It is reused here and also sold all over the country," says Weil.

# Why did the Italians seek high ground?

**Topography contributed to this St. Louis neighborhood's nickname.**

The nineteenth century saw the discovery of large clay deposits beneath much of southwest St. Louis. Landmarks Association of St. Louis executive director Andrew Weil says the clay was suitable for making bricks. It wasn't long before brick production facilities opened in the area.

As the twentieth century approached, European immigrants arrived in St. Louis in search of a new life. Numerous Italians were drawn by the prospects of clay and brick work. Many settled nearby on what was the most elevated ground in St. Louis, an area later dubbed the Hill.

Clay jobs were plentiful. Workers sent word to their families and friends about the opportunities in St. Louis. Newcomers arrived and settled on the Hill, and the Italian neighborhood grew. They brought with them their food, culture, and a strong sense of community.

**WHERE WE LIVE**

More than a hundred years later, that close-knit neighborhood bond remains. Many who live on the Hill are lifelong residents, as were their parents and grandparents. The neighborhood's many restaurants feature savory foods prepared using treasured family recipes. It's an epicurean's delight. Benvenuti a St. Louis!

# Fact BOX

The Hill's streets are narrow, lined with rows of small, tidy houses and yards. The Hill's unique fire hydrants are painted red, white, and green and resemble the Italian flag.

THE ITALIAN IMMIGRANTS

# What's up with all the four-family flats?

Drive around St. Louis and you'll see them. They're the brick residences with multiple front doors. St. Louisans call them flats, and they house multiple family units.

St. Louis was an important industrial city by the late 1800s. Its proximity to the Mississippi and Missouri Rivers, plus its position as a crossroads for multiple railroads, made it an ideal location for business development. Business growth meant the need for additional workers, and workers needed places to live.

"St. Louis was a huge city," says Andrew Weil, executive director of the Landmarks Association of St. Louis. "Flats became popular in middle- and working-class neighborhoods in the early twentieth century where space was at a premium."

Numerous St. Louis streets are lined with brick flats. "Often if a family could afford to build a residence, they'd build one with an extra unit for rental, which would provide additional income," says the Landmarks Association's Rick Rosen. "It didn't cost that much more to build a multiple-family than a single-family home."

**WHERE WE LIVE**

Multiple-unit housing can be found in other large cities. "Cleveland, Baltimore, and Cambridge, Massachusetts, have them," says Rosen. "What's unique about St. Louis is the amount of detail work on even the most modest dwellings. The labor and craftsmanship were highly skilled. The humblest houses resemble palaces in the details and embellishments."

# Fact BOX

Many European immigrants who settled here had limited formal education but amazing artistic building skills. Structures they created at the turn of the nineteenth century were functional as well as beautiful, featuring terra-cotta enhancements and statuary.

Other talented St. Louis artisans specialized in an architectural embellishment style called sgrafitto or sgraffiti. The production of sgrafitto involves a centuries-old method of applying tinted cement plaster in layers. This technique was popularized during Italy's Renaissance. In the United States, sgrafitto was found almost exclusively in St. Louis, thanks to resident Italian immigrant artists.

Buildings in the 600 block of Olive Street feature interesting terra-cotta. They are included in the Olive Street Terra Cotta District, a part of the National Register of Historic Places.

# You call these skyscrapers?

## St. Louis—a leader in architectural style

St. Louis may not be home to the world's tallest skyscrapers, but the 1891 Louis H. Sullivan–designed, ten-story Wainwright Building was the first tall office building of its kind.

"The Wainwright Building was unique in that the exterior masonry was supported by a steel frame," says Rick Rosen of the Landmarks Association. "Height wasn't the goal here. It was

**WHERE WE LIVE**

the building's vertical aesthetics. The aesthetics expressed that this was a new and different office building. It had very dramatic vertical shafts, with shadow and light demonstrating the tallness of the building, not that it was the tallest building. The Wainwright Building broke

completely and cleanly with the architectural trends of the past."

St. Louisan Ellis Wainwright was a wealthy businessman, a patron of great architecture as well as of the modern and unique. Sullivan's fresh ideas were intriguing, so Wainwright secured him to design his St. Louis office building. The result was a structure that pleased Wainwright and earned Sullivan accolades. He was given the unofficial title, "father of modern American architecture."

The Wainwright Building was listed on the National Register of Historic Places in 1968 and today houses state of Missouri offices.

Fact BOX

The thirteen-floor Civil Courts Building on North Tucker Boulevard looks like two distinct buildings—one on top of the other. The top section is a replica of the tomb of King Mausolus (one of the Seven Wonders of the Ancient World) built in Asia Minor in 352 B.C. It features thirty-two Ionic columns (eight on each side) and a pyramid-shaped roof topped with two sphinxlike creatures sporting St. Louis's symbol, the fleur-de-lis. The building was constructed between 1928 and 1930, a time when architects looked to ancient structures for design ideas. The building houses a law library.

# Wait . . . you had to leave home to take a bath?

## St. Louis's municipal bathhouses

St. Louis was the fourth-largest city in the country. It also was a stinky, dirty place. Waste disposal, sanitation, and hygiene were primitive.

Few houses had running water or tubs. Bathing required multiple trips to an outdoor water source and heating water before dumping it into a washtub. If the household included multiple generations, they often used the same bath water.

Social reformers sought to improve living conditions in large cities, including promoting cleanliness. This led to construction of public bathhouses, but St. Louis was slow to join the public bath movement.

**WHERE WE LIVE**

Public Bath House No. 1 opened here in August 1907 with separate facilities for men and women. There was no charge to use the bathhouse. Soap and towels could be rented if not brought from home. The concept was declared a success, with more than five hundred thousand people using the facility by 1915. Five additional bathhouses were built in St. Louis. The last one, built in 1937, remained open until 1965. It still stands near the popular Crown Candy Kitchen.

**Fact BOX**

Outdoor privies played no small role in St. Louis's odiferous atmosphere. At that time, only the wealthy had indoor toilets. Certain neighborhoods northwest of downtown were densely populated, with several generations of a family sharing one living space. A quick-fix solution was to build multiple-level yard toilets. Crudely made of wood and scrap metal, these structures sat two and three levels high, with toilet chambers positioned atop each other. A multilevel privy vault might serve up to eighty individuals.

# Why does St. Louis have a large Bosnian population?

## Welcome to St. Louis, Missouri, USA

St. Louis has been and continues to be made up of an ethnically diverse population. During its early years as a fur-trading village, French and Spanish transplants roamed the streets along with Native Americans.

The nineteenth century saw an influx of tens of thousands of new citizens from Germany and Ireland. Oppression, famine, persecution, and poor living conditions in their native countries drove many to seek the freedoms and new life available in the United States and ultimately St. Louis. Citizens of other European countries followed, including Greeks, Syrians, and Asians. They brought with them their customs, foods, skills, and religious beliefs. By the end of the nineteenth century, St. Louis was the fourth-largest city in the United States and one of the most ethnically diverse.

 **WHERE WE LIVE**

And the resettlement trend has continued. In the early 1990s, violence, torture, ethnic cleansing, and mass genocide resulted in thousands of deaths and the displacement of several million Bosnians. Few of those who escaped the horrors and survived were not impacted by the death of one or more family members or friends.

Once again, St. Louis welcomed and assimilated an ethnic group in need of a new home. Affordable housing and work opportunities were big draws. Many Bosnian refugees settled in South St. Louis near historic Bevo Mill. Today, St. Louis's Bosnian community is estimated to number approximately seventy thousand, the largest Bosnian population outside of Bosnia. Numerous businesses, restaurants, mosques, language classes, and a newspaper have been established to meet the needs of the area's growing Bosnian American population.

**Fact BOX**

The Bosnia Memory Project at St. Louis's Fontbonne University strives to maintain a lasting record of St. Louis Bosnian genocide survivors' experiences. The goal is to collect oral histories, personal accounts, written materials, and photographs in order to increase community awareness and education. The National Endowment for the Humanities awarded a $100,000 matching grant to the project. The university also offers classes and events related to Bosnian history and culture.

# The spirit of flight

## St. Louis's aeronautical connection

St. Louis has a long history of involvement with aeronautics. "St. Louis was important to aviation and aviation was important to St. Louis," says attorney and author Alan Hoffman, an advocate for the aviation legacy of St. Louis.

According to Hoffman, St. Louis played a major role in many aviation industry "firsts." St. Louisan Albert Bond Lambert was friends with American and European balloonists and aircraft pioneers, took flying lessons with the famous Wright brothers, and created the earliest St. Louis area airports (St. Louis's current airport bears his name).

Glenn Curtiss made the first flight in St. Louis at Forest Park in October 1909. In 1910, President Theodore Roosevelt came to St. Louis to attend the International Air Tournament. The tournament attracted leading American and foreign aviators and airplane builders. Roosevelt was invited to fly with a young pilot, accepted the invitation on the spot, and became the first U.S. president to fly.

 **UP IN THE AIR**

Thomas Benoist, an early aircraft builder, designed and built an airplane in University City in 1910 and opened a flying school at Kinloch Field in 1911. In March 1912, Albert Berry made the first parachute descent from an airplane at Jefferson Barracks.

St. Louis was also part of the original transcontinental post office air mail network established in 1920. The city's hosting of the 1923 International Air Races (facilitated by Lambert) attracted a young aviator named Charles Lindbergh, who in 1926 established the air mail route between St. Louis and Chicago. It was here that Lindbergh met local business leaders who eventually sponsored his historic non-stop flight between New York and Paris in 1927. In appreciation, he named his aircraft the *Spirit of St. Louis.*

"St. Louis has been a major aircraft production center since 1927 when the Curtiss-Robertson Company was established at Lambert, becoming the predecessor of Curtiss-Wright, McDonnell Aircraft, McDonnell-Douglas, and Boeing," says Hoffman. "Boeing continues to build the F-15 Eagle, F/A-18 Super Hornet, and EA-18G Growler jet aircraft for the U.S. and its allies."

**Fact BOX**

Lambert–St. Louis Flying Field opened in 1923. Lambert–St. Louis Municipal Airport was established in 1928. It hired the first air traffic controller, Archie League. Military aviation began here in 1923 with the establishment of a National Guard unit at Lambert. Parts of the *Mercury* and *Gemini* spacecraft were designed and constructed in St. Louis.

# My beautiful balloon

## St. Louis's love of hot-air balloons

St. Louis has a long history with hot-air balloons. Beginning in the late 1800s, hot-air balloonists came to St. Louis for demonstrations. Then, as now, the balloons drew crowds of observers.

It's a calm, sunny afternoon in Forest Park, St. Louis's largest urban park. The park's Central Field is alive with noise and activity as crew members inflate seventy-plus tethered hot-air balloons. The colorful fabrics unfurl as flames and gasses lift the balloons to an upright position.

Suddenly a single balloon rises above the tree line. Prevailing winds carry the lead balloon and its passengers toward South St. Louis. Soon the other balloons' tethering ropes are released and . . . they're off! The Great Forest Park Balloon Race has begun as it has for the last forty-plus years.

UP IN THE AIR

Each September thousands of spectators and certified balloonists from around the country jam the park to witness one of the nation's oldest, biggest, free urban hot-air balloon events.

No two balloons are alike. Some bear colorful corporate identification; others are uniquely shaped. Balloonists attempt to follow the lead balloon and land as close to it as possible when it descends. Spectators of all ages love to watch them.

A balloon glow is held in the park the night before the race. It allows spectators to get an up-close look at the nighttime beauty of the lighted tethered balloons.

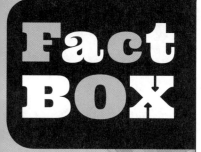

**Fact BOX**

It was 1909, and St. Louis had been incorporated as a city for a hundred years. This called for a celebration, or multiple celebrations. One of the celebratory spectacles was a balloon race. Hot-air balloons were gathered near one of Laclede Gas Light Company's huge coal gas holders (also called a gasometer or gas reservoir) near Forest Park. The *St. Louis-Post Dispatch* estimated that approximately one hundred thousand people watched the "gasbags" take flight. Then, as now, St. Louisans loved a good public party.

# This city is fairly infatuated with 1904.

It was 1904 and St. Louis was about to hit the international stage.

After months of negotiating, planning, building, and improving, the Louisiana Purchase Exposition was about to open. Everything from water purification to transportation of people from foreign cultures had been considered. And this was before the days of mass communication and technology. Would the fair begin without a glitch?

"The fair was originally scheduled for 1903 to commemorate the centennial of the Louisiana Purchase but was delayed to allow more companies and countries to participate," says Max Storm, founder of the 1904 World's Fair Society. "To get started, the city put up $5 million, the federal government put up $5 million, and fair organizers sold $5 million in fair stock. It was the only world's fair in history that paid for itself."

Washington University, which planned to relocate from downtown to its current site adjacent to Forest Park, delayed moving into thirteen new buildings so the structures could be used during the fair. "Brookings Hall was the fair's administration building," says Storm.

Most of the fair's buildings were designed to be temporary and were removed after the fair. Exceptions were a section of today's Saint Louis Art Museum and the Saint Louis Zoo's flight cage, which was a Smithsonian Institution exhibit. The fair closed after seven months and approximately twenty million visitors.

And contrary to popular opinion, hot dogs, ice cream cones, and iced tea were not invented at the fair. "They were popularized at the fair but not invented there," says Storm. "Puffed rice was introduced at the fair."

# Fact Box

The fair's end was just the beginning of Forest Park, an urban oasis where generations of St. Louisans continue to enjoy beauty and amenities. The admission-free Saint Louis Zoo, Art Museum, and Missouri History Museum attract visitors year-round. The outdoor Municipal Opera (now called the Muny) has been hosting live summer stage performances since it opened in 1919. The Jewel Box, opened in 1936, is a gardener's delight. During winter months, Steinberg Memorial Skating Rink (opened in 1957) attracts ice skating enthusiasts of all ages. When the St. Louis area gets a good blanket of snow, Art Hill, the best sledding hill in town, is dotted with winter enthusiasts riding on everything from snow boards to cafeteria trays. Forest Park has a challenging public golf course, and paved trails around the park host joggers, walkers, and bicyclists each day.

# St. Louis really hosted an Olympics?

## St. Louis's Olympic connection

Hosting the Summer Olympics is a big deal. Countries spend big bucks trying to persuade the Olympic Committee to choose them as the host venue.

Once upon a time (1904 to be exact), the Summer Olympics were hosted in St. Louis. The timing coincided nicely with the World's Fair. It was indeed the year the world came to St. Louis. And the best part was that St. Louis beat out Chicago as the host city.

"The St. Louis Olympics was only the third such modern-day competition," says Max Storm, founder of the 1904 World's Fair Society. "And only four U.S. cities have ever held the Olympics. Chicago wanted the Olympics, had approval to hold it, but St. Louis

**THE FAIR**

threatened to overshadow Chicago's games by hosting more events tied to the World's Fair. Chicago decided to let the games be held here."

Several structures remain from the 1904 Olympics and are part of Washington University. The concrete stadium and stands, plus the school's track, were used during the competition. Parts of a nearby building also were used.

Then, as now, there was controversy. One participant cheated. Another ingested a substance to enhance his performance.

**Fact BOX**

George Coleman Poage earned a bachelor's degree in history from the University of Wisconsin. While attending college, he had been a hurdler and sprinter for the school's track team. He traveled to St. Louis in 1904 to represent the Milwaukee Athletic Club in the Olympic Games. Poage finished third in the 400-meter hurdles and third in the 200-meter hurdles the following day, winning two bronze medals. He was the first African American to earn an Olympic medal.

# *Turn right* at the Catholic church. *No, not that one, the other one.*

## The St. Louis Catholic connection

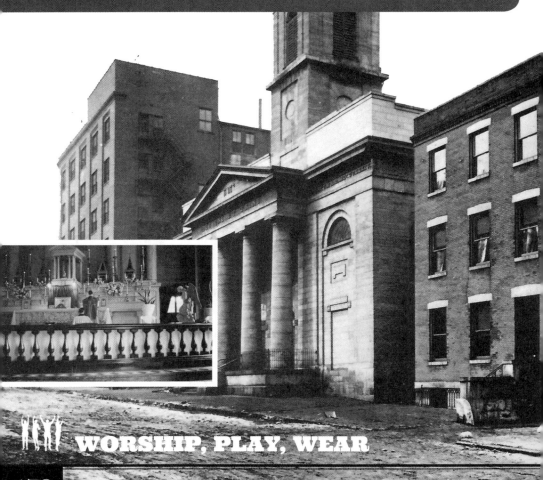

**WORSHIP, PLAY, WEAR**

St. Louis founders Pierre Laclede and August Chouteau were of French descent. They also were devout Catholics. Building a house of worship here was a priority. The site they dedicated in 1764 sat near the banks of the Mississippi River.

Today that site still houses a Catholic church (the fourth on the site)—the Basilica of Saint Louis, King of France, named in honor of France's King Louis IX. "It was the first Catholic cathedral west of the Mississippi River, it's the oldest building in the city of St. Louis, and it's the only piece of riverfront property that remains in the hands of its original owner—the Archdiocese of St. Louis," says archdiocese spokesperson Gabe Jones.

And as the population of St. Louis grew and expanded from the original riverfront settlement, so too did the Catholic Church. The Archdiocese of St. Louis oversees the operations of the parishes and schools in the city of St. Louis as well as in ten surrounding counties. "The archdiocese has approximately 180 parishes and a network of one-hundred-plus schools," Jones says. "Throughout European history, the French had a profound effect on the Catholic Church. Some of that connection remains in St. Louis."

# Fact BOX

The Basilica of Saint Louis, King of France, the Parish of St. Louis (a.k.a. the Old Cathedral), was built between 1831 and 1834 with twelve-hundred-pound blocks of granite. And this was long before the invention of bulldozers and forklifts.

# This town looks sleepy for a Saturday night.

**Some St. Louis neighborhoods come to life after dark.**

**WORSHIP, PLAY, WEAR**

Think St. Louisans roll up the sidewalks after dark? Think again.

St. Louis neighborhoods like the Loop (University City), Washington Avenue (downtown), the Central West End, South Grand Avenue, the Grove, and Soulard (South City) are self-contained dining and entertainment districts. Restaurants, bars, breweries, theaters, performing venues, and pubs abound. The party's just starting when the sun goes down.

In the mood for something sophisticated? Catch a performance at Powell Symphony Hall, the Fabulous Fox, or the Peabody Opera House.

Thirsty? St. Louis has a dozen breweries both large and small, with selections ranging from wheat brews to lagers. "We market to people who like good beer," says Urban Chestnut's Florian Kuplent.

Want to dance? St. Louis is home to an array of nightclubs where you can dance the night away.

Hungry? St. Louis has a diverse population, so one-of-a-kind ethnic restaurants are plentiful. Or try a pub specializing in authentic Irish food.

Want to listen to smooth jazz or karaoke? St. Louis has both covered at multiple locations.

Need to check on your favorite teams? St. Louis is a sports town, and sports bars are plentiful.

How about topping off the night with a dessert martini or a sweet confection? Uptown sophistication or down-home charm, you have choices.

In search of quiet, intimate surroundings or cozy atmosphere? They're here too.

# St. Louis nightlife is happening!
## Just ask a local for suggestions.

# Over one hundred years old, but still called new?

The Catholic Church has been an integral part of St. Louis since its founding in 1764. An early structure erected by the French settlers was a house (actually more of a shed) of worship. That riverfront site today is occupied by the Cathedral Basilica of Saint Louis, King of France, the Parish of St. Louis. Its stately spire is dwarfed by its neighbor, the Gateway Arch.

St. Louis's population grew and expanded westward. By the start of the twentieth century, plans were made for the construction of an artistic masterpiece, a Catholic place of worship unlike anything nearby. The massive granite structure was to be built in sections and covered inside with mosaics and stained glass windows. Construction of the Cathedral Basilica of Saint Louis took years to complete (ground clearing, 1907; first mass, 1914; consecration, 1926), with artisans brought in from Europe. Locals soon referred to it as the New Cathedral and the original riverfront church as the Old Cathedral.

 **WORSHIP, PLAY, WEAR**

The New Cathedral contains a spectacular display of eighty-three million individual mosaic tiles. The tiles depict scenes from stories in the Bible. "The elaborate mosaics bring a little bit of Europe to St. Louis," says Cathedral Basilica spokesperson Nicole Heerlein. "They are monuments to the test of time, built to the glory of God. We attract tourists, but the buildings are first and foremost a sacred and religious base for St. Louis Catholics."

## Fact BOX

St. Louis is unique in that both the Old Cathedral (circa 1830s) and the New Cathedral (early 1900s) have been designated by the pope in Rome as basilicas. Only those Catholic churches with spiritual or historical significance are given this distinction. "It's not all that common to have two basilicas in one city," says Gabe Jones, Archdiocese of St. Louis spokesperson.

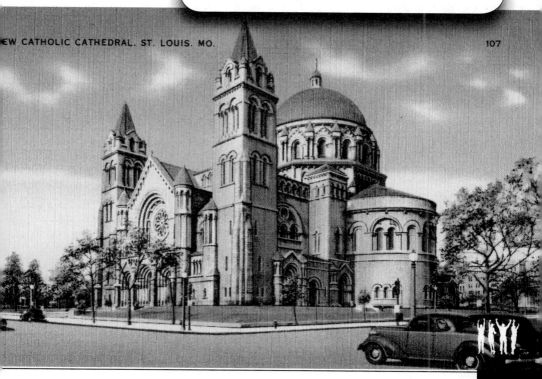

EW CATHOLIC CATHEDRAL. ST. LOUIS. MO.    107

# What is HOLY CORNERS?

## Houses of worship + beautiful architecture = timeless beauty

Step back in time. Downtown St. Louis has become too dirty, noisy, and commercial for wealthy St. Louisans. Enclaves like Lucas Place and Vandeventer Place have fallen out of favor. Time to move west.

The rich build fine mansions in an area called the Central West End near Forest Park. The area is sure to be the next up-and-coming residential utopia. And if a large contingent of the population is moving west, so too are some of the houses of worship and private organizations.

Then, as now, Kingshighway was a major thoroughfare. Open land was available where it intersected with Washington Boulevard—the perfect location for churches and gathering spots. From 1902 through 1908, construction crews created magnificent structures designed by famed architects. St. John's Methodist Church was designed by Theodore C. Link, designer of Union Station and other notable buildings. It was completed in 1902. First Church of Christ, Scientist, relocated from downtown in 1904, moving into a building designed by the firm Mauran, Russell and Garden.

 **WORSHIP, PLAY, WEAR**

Unlike other nearby structures, the Racquet Club was not built to house a religious organization. It was designed by Mauran, Russell and Garden and opened in 1906 as an athletic club for nearby homeowners. In 1907, the congregation of Second Baptist Church moved from downtown into a new neighboring structure also designed by Mauran, Russell and Garden. The architectural firm Barnett, Haynes and Barnett designed a Roman/Corinthian building for Temple Israel, which relocated from downtown in 1908. The final structure considered to be part of the Holy Corners complex was the Tuscan Masonic Temple, which faces Westminster Place. It was designed by Albert B. Groves and dedicated in 1908.

The concentration of houses of worship around the Kingshighway/Washington Boulevard intersection soon led to the area's nickname, Holy Corners.

Fast forward to 2018. The buildings remain, but they've been repurposed or are occupied by different congregations. The area is a National Register Historic District.

## Fact Box

The Racquet Club was created by young businessmen wanting to participate in sports and be close to home. In 1927, a group of men at the club made an important decision. They agreed to spend $10,000 to back a young aviator on a nonstop flight from New York to Paris. The aviator was Charles Lindbergh, who named his plane the *Spirit of St. Louis*.

# St. Louis is a party city? Welcome to Party Town!

Saint Patrick's Day Procession in Saint Louis 1874

## St. Louisans love a good civic party or parade or reason to celebrate.

When it comes to parties for, say, thousands, St. Louis has it covered. Parties, parades, festivals, and civic celebrations of any kind are enjoyed by St. Louisans of all ages. We're a party town!

St. Louis's celebration of Mardi Gras has become legendary, with two distinct parades. The Grande Parade features floats, krewes, and beads. The Barkus Pet Parade features hundreds of costumed dogs and their owners, plus an occasional pink poodle.

Each March, St. Louis hosts not one but two St. Patrick's Day parades. Both claim to be the official St. Patrick's Day Parade. It doesn't matter. We love them both. Marching bands, balloons, floats, and thousands of spectators. Even if you're ancestors weren't Irish, it's still a good time.

Other annual celebrations include the LouFest Music Festival, Octoberfest and the celebration of all things German, the St. Nicholas Greek Festival, the Missouri Botanical Garden's Japanese Festival, and the Fourth of July's Fair Saint Louis.

**WORSHIP, PLAY, WEAR**

And how did St. Louis become such a festival-loving city? "St. Louis has always been known as a drinking city, what with all the breweries through the years," says *St. Louis Post-Dispatch* columnist Joe Holleman. "But the large-scale celebrations are something relatively new in the last thirty or so years."

**Fact BOX**

In 2018, Fair Saint Louis announced that America's Biggest Birthday Party (celebrating the Fourth of July) was returning to its original home near the Arch. The green space surrounding the Arch (formerly the Jefferson National Expansion Memorial) has been recreated and renamed Gateway Arch National Park. The reconfigured area features a new museum beneath the Arch, plus the park now connects to the Old Courthouse grounds.

# Where the wares were wearable.

## St. Louis's connection to the shoe and clothing industries

For many decades, St. Louis was a major hub for shoe and clothing design and production. It was ideally located in the center of the United States, with ready access to railroad and river transportation. That meant raw materials (leather, fur pelts) and finished products could enter and leave St. Louis in an efficient manner.

Much of the production and warehouse activity of St. Louis's garment district centered around Washington Avenue. By the 1920s, the garment district encompassed fifteen blocks. Many yesteryear industrial facilities continue to line the busy thoroughfare today but have been repurposed into loft living and office spaces. However, for many years the area was electric with the activity of thousands of workers, the hum of automated machines, and delivery vehicles.

Dozens of shoe manufacturers and their headquarters buildings were located in St. Louis, including International Shoe Company; Brown Shoe; Edison Brothers; Friedman-Shelby; Roberts, Johnson & Rand; and Fox-Wohl.

 **WORSHIP, PLAY, WEAR**

Seventy-four garment companies called St. Louis home, including manufacturers of coats, dress shirts, hats, dresses, neckwear, wedding gowns, sleepwear, and lingerie. Innovations born in St. Louis included junior-size clothing and ready-to-wear fashions.

Shannon Meyer is senior curator with the Missouri History Museum. The museum's textile collections include hundreds of clothing items manufactured in St. Louis, some over one hundred years old and in pristine condition. "The History Museum has an amazing collection." she says.

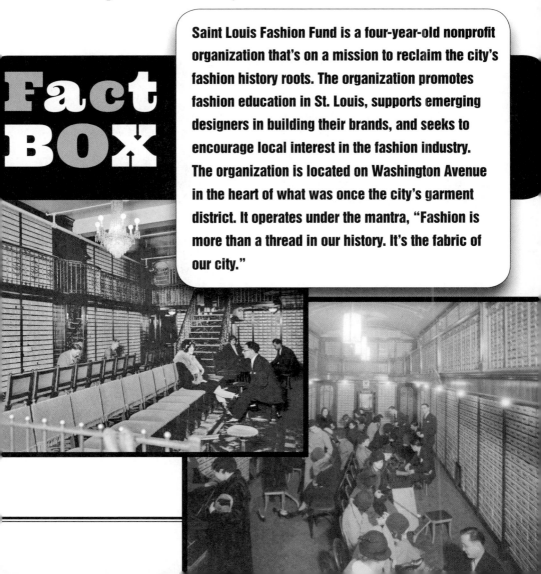

**Fact BOX**

Saint Louis Fashion Fund is a four-year-old nonprofit organization that's on a mission to reclaim the city's fashion history roots. The organization promotes fashion education in St. Louis, supports emerging designers in building their brands, and seeks to encourage local interest in the fashion industry. The organization is located on Washington Avenue in the heart of what was once the city's garment district. It operates under the mantra, "Fashion is more than a thread in our history. It's the fabric of our city."

# BIBLIOGRAPHY

## Books

Auble, John. *A History of St. Louis Gangsters*. St. Louis, MO: National Crime Research Society, 2000.

Barley, Patricia and Woods, Joan. *Missouri Life—Special World's Fair Anniversary Edition*, "The Greatest of Expositions." Jefferson City, MO: May-August 1979.

Baugher, David. *Secret St. Louis—A Guide to the Weird, Wonderful and Obscure*. St. Louis, MO: Reedy Press, 2016.

Berger, Henry W. *St. Louis and Empire: 250 Years of Imperial Quest and Urban Crisis*. Carbondale, IL: Southern Illinois University Press, 2015.

Bremer, Jeff. *A Store Almost in Sight*. Iowa City, IA: University of Iowa Press, 2014.

Conard, Howard L. *Encyclopedia of the History of Missouri Railroad Articles*. St. Louis, MO: Southern History Company, 1901.

Cox, Jeremy R.C. *St. Louis Aviation*. Charleston, SC: Arcadia Publishing, 2011.

Dobney, Frederick J. *River Engineers on the Middle Mississippi: A History of the St. Louis District, U.S. Army Corps of Engineers*. Washington, D.C.: U.S. Government Printing Office, 1976.

Dry, Camille N. *Pictorial St. Louis, the Great Metropolis of the Mississippi Valley: A Topographical Survey Drawn in Perspective, A.D. 1875*. Designed and edited by Richard J. Compton. St. Louis, MO: Knight Publishing, 1979.

Erwin, James W. *The Homefront in Civil War Missouri*. Charleston, SC: The History Press, 2014.

Erwin, Vicki Berger. *Kirkwood*. Charleston, SC: Arcadia Publishing, 2013.

Evans, Mike. *The Blues—A Visual History, 100 Years of Music that Changed the World*. New York, NY: Sterling, 2014.

Faherty, William Barnaby. *The Saint Louis Portrait*. Tulsa, OK: Continental Heritage, Inc., 1978.

Fox, Tim, editor. *Where We Live—A Guide To St. Louis Communities*. St. Louis, MO: Missouri Historical Society Press, 1995.

Gerteis, Louis S. *Civil War St. Louis*. Lawrence, KS: University Press of Kansas, 2001.

Gill, McCune. *The St. Louis Story*. St. Louis, MO: Historical Record Association, 1952.

Hannon, Robert E., editor. *St. Louis: Its Neighborhoods and Neighbors, Landmarks and Milestones*. St. Louis, MO: Buxton & Skinner Printing, 1985.

Harris, Nini. *Downtown St. Louis*. St. Louis, MO: Reedy Press, 2015.

Horgan, James J. *City of Flight*. Gerald, MO: The Patrice Press, 1984.

Hyde, William and Conard, Howard L., editors. *Encyclopedia of the History of St. Louis, Vol. IV.* The Southern History Company, 1899.

Jones, H.M. *Police Guide and Directory of St. Louis.* St. Louis, MO: Metropolitan Police Force, 1884.

Kavanaugh, Maureen. *Hidden History of St. Louis.* St. Louis, MO: The History Press, 2017.

Kimbrough, Mary and Dagen, Margaret W. *Victory Without Violence.* Columbia, MO: University of Missouri Press, 2000.

Lange, Dave. *Soccer Made in St. Louis: A History of the Game in America's First Soccer Capital.* St. Louis, MO: Reedy Press, 2011.

Leonard, Mary Delach. *Animals Always—100 Years of the Saint Louis Zoo.* Columbia, MO: University of Missouri Press, 2009.

Lester, Julius. *The Blues Singers: Ten Who Rocked the World.* New York, NY: Hyperion Books for Children, 2001

Magnan, William B. *Streets of St. Louis.* Groton, CT: Right Press, Inc., 1994.

Miller, Howard S. *The Eads Bridge—James Buchanan Eads.* St. Louis, MO: Missouri Historical Society Press, 1999.

Mormino, Gary Ross. *Immigrants on the Hill: Italian Americans in St. Louis 1882-1982.* Chicago, IL: University of Illinois Press, 1986.

Mouser, Bruce L., emeritus professor of history, University of Wisconsin-La Crosse. *George Coleman—1880-1962, America's First African American Olympic Medalist: A Biography.* La Crosse, WI: Self-published, 2017.

Neiman, John. *In Concert: KSHE and 40+ Years of ROCK in St. Louis.* Des Plaines, IL: Big Jack Publishing, 2009.

O'Neil, Tim. *Mobs, Mayhem & Murder: Tales from the St. Louis Police Department.* St. Louis, MO: St. Louis Post-Dispatch Books, 2009.

O'Neil, Tim. *The Gateway Arch—An Unlikely Masterpiece.* St. Louis, MO: St. Louis Post-Dispatch Books, 2015.

Pfeiffer, David A. *Bridging the Mississippi: The Railroads and Steamboats Clash at the Rock Island Bridge.* Washington, D.C.: National Archives Prologue Magazine, 2004.

Primm, James Neal. *Lion of the Valley.* St. Louis, MO: Pruett Publishing, 1981.

Sandweiss, Eric. *St. Louis—The Evolution of an American Urban Landscape.* Philadelphia, PA: Temple University Press, 2001.

Santelli, Robert; George-Warren, Holly; Brown, Jim, editors. *American Roots Music.* New York, NY: Henry N. Abrams, Incorporated, 2001.

Scharf, Thomas. *History of Saint Louis City and County from the Earliest Periods to the Present Day.* Philadelphia, PA: Louis H. Everts & Co., 1883.

Sharoff, Robert. *American City: St. Louis Architecture.* Mulgrave, Vic.: The Images Publishing Group, 2011.

Shepley, Carol Ferring. *Movers and Shakers. Scalawags and Suffragettes. Tales From Bellefontaine Cemetery*. St. Louis, MO: University of Missouri Press, 2008.

Spencer, Thomas M. *The St. Louis Veiled Prophet Celebration—Power on Parade, 1877-1995*. Columbia, MO: University of Missouri Press, 2000.

Stadler, Frances Herd. *St. Louis Day By Day*. St. Louis, MO: The Patrice Press, 1989.

Stepenoff, Bonnie. *The Dead End Kids of St. Louis*. Columbia, MO: University of Missouri Press, 2010.

Stage, Wm. *Fading Signs of St. Louis*. Charleston, SC: The History Press, 2013.

Stage, Wm. *Ghost Signs: Brick Wall Signs in America*. Cincinnati, Ohio: Signs of the Times Publishing Company, 1989.

Stevens, Walter B. *St. Louis: The Fourth City*. Chicago, IL: S.J. Clarke Publishing Company, 1909.

Terry, Elizabeth; Wright, John; McCarthy, Patrick. *Ethnic St. Louis*. St. Louis, MO: Webster University Press, Reedy Press, 2015.

Toft, Carolyn Hewes. *St. Louis: Landmarks and Historic Districts*. St. Louis, MO: Landmarks Association of St. Louis, 1988.

Toft, Carolyn Hewes. *The Hill: The Ethnic Heritage of an Urban Neighborhood*. St. Louis, MO: Ethnic Heritage Study Council, 1980.

Vollmar, Joseph E., Jr. *James B. Eads and the Great St. Louis Bridge*. St. Louis, MO: The Engineers' Club of St. Louis, 1974.

Winter, William C. *The Civil War in St. Louis—A Guided Tour*. St. Louis, MO: Missouri Historical Society Press, 1994.

Woodcock, Jim. *St. Louis Blues Hockey Club 1967-2002: Note by Note*. St. Louis, MO: Pinnacle Press, 2002.

Young, Andrew D. *Streets and Streetcars of St. Louis: A Sentimental Journey*. St. Louis, MO: Archway Publishing, 2002.

## Newspapers & Other Materials

"Advertising Cards (late 19thcentury, early 20th century)--St. Louis, MO," Missouri History Museum printed materials archives. Viewed July 31, 2015.

Allen, Michael R. "Finding Dr. Martin Luther King, Jr. in St. Louis," Preservation Research Office newsletter, St. Louis, MO, January 21, 2013.

Arnold, Willis Ryder. "'Unfortunately Help Always Comes a Little Too Late:' St. Louis Bosnians Remember Srebrenica Massacre." St. Louis Public Radio KWMU broadcast, July 11, 2015.

Batts, Jeannette. "A Sewer Runs Through It," *Riverfront Times*, Dec. 6, 2000.

Beauchamp, Scott. "The Mystery of St. Louis's Veiled Prophet," *The Atlantic*, Sept. 2, 2014.

Berry, Emanuele. "Bosnians in St. Louis Struggle Over Identity, Provide Lesson on 'Tragic Optimism,'" St. Louis Public Radio KWMU broadcast, April 15, 2015.

Brown, Lisa. "Schlafly Beer Is 'Recalibrating For Growth,'" *St. Louis Post-Dispatch*, Jan 16, 2016.

Brown, Lisa. "Urban Chestnut To Open Research Brewery," *St. Louis Post-Dispatch*, Jan. 12, 2016.

Cassella, William N., Jr. "City-County Separation: The Great Divorce of 1876," *Missouri Historical Society Bulletin*, Jan. 1959.

Chen, Eli. "After 'Atomic Homefront' Release, Frustrated Residents Fill Army Corps Coldwater Creek Meeting." St. Louis Public Radio KWMU broadcast, Feb. 23, 2018.

Christo, Bethany; Cothran, Shannon; Miller, Liz; Veety, Andrew Mark. "Meat+Carbs=Slingers," *Feast Magazine*, Aug. 28, 2014.

Climate Change and Your Health-St. Louis & Columbia, MO. "Heat in the Heartland." (brochure, date and author unknown).

Collins, Cameron. "The History of the St. Louis Municipal Bath House." *nextSTL*, Dec. 20, 2012.

"Gold medal from 1904 St. Louis Olympics sells for $125K," *St. Louis Post-Dispatch*, June 14, 2018.

Graham, Sara. "6 Best Doughnut Shops In St. Louis," *Riverfront Times*, Jan. 22, 2015.

"Cultural Resource Survey-Old Dutchtown and Benton Park West Survey." Prepared for The City of St. Louis, Missouri, by Historic Preservation Services, LLC. Aug. 30, 2003.

Eschner, Kat. "The Budweiser Clydesdales' First Gig Was the End of Prohibition." Smithsonianmag.com, March 28, 2017.

Feldt, Brian. "You Can't Move In Until 2020, but Cardinals Start Pre-Leasing Apartments at Ballpark Village." *St. Louis Post-Dispatch*, Feb. 13, 2018.

Flood, Amelia. "Words from Home: Newspapers." St. Louis Public Radio KWMU broadcast Oct. 8, 2017.

"Guide-Map St. Louis and Vicinity" St. Louis Public Service Company, 1948.

Graham, Bill. "Snowy Owls from Arctic Making a Winter Visit to Missouri," Missouri Department of Conservation news release, Dec. 22, 2017.

Gray, Bryce. "Dredging the Past," *St. Louis Post-Dispatch*, June 3, 2018.

"History of the Saint Louis Zoo Board Book," with unknown author, printed booklet, 2015.

Hahn, Valerie Schremp. "A Saint, a Relic and a Miracle in St. Louis: Descendants Gather to Celebrate," *St. Louis Post-Dispatch*, March 18, 2018.

Hahn, Valerie Schremp. "New Arch Museum Honoring St. Louis' Dynamic History," *St. Louis Post-Dispatch*, Feb. 1, 2018.

Holleman, Joe. "Spotlight: Last Indian Mound In St. Louis Still Deteriorating," *St. Louis Post-Dispatch*, Oct. 4, 2015.

Holleman, Joe. "Long, Troubled History For Lindbergh Boulevard," *St. Louis Post-Dispatch*, March 5, 2016.

Holleman, Joe. "KSHE's 50th birthday shows on Tuesday will feature 'rocktogenarian' Ruth Hutchinson," *St. Louis Post-Dispatch*, Nov. 7, 2017.

"Holy Corners." U.S. Department of the Interior, National Park Service, National Register of Historic Places Inventory. Prepared by W.G. Seibert, Heritage/St. Louis, January 3, 1975.

Heuer, Alex. "Former Military Commander Mladic's Genocide Verdict Hits Home in St. Louis' Bosnian Community." St. Louis Public Radio KWMU broadcast Nov. 22, 2017.

Jarrett, Linda. "Uncover The Tales Of Missouri's Cemeteries," *AAA Midwest Traveler*, September/October 2015.

Kehe, Marjorie. "Entrepreneur Joe Edwards helps make St. Louis vibrant again," *The Christian Science Monitor*, Dec. 14, 2012.

Krystal, Becky. "Impulsive Traveler: Eagle Watching in Grafton, Ill.," *Washington Post*, Jan. 14, 2011.

Lang, Edward. "Arch Triumph," *Missouri Life Magazine*, June/July 2018.

Leonard, Mary Delach. "These Historical Photos Show How Much St. Louis Has Changed." St. Louis Public Radio KWMU broadcast May 7, 2014.

"Looking at the history of streetcars in St. Louis," *St. Louis Post-Dispatch*, March 5, 2017.

Luebbering, Dr. Ken. "Missouri's Germans and the Civil War," Missouri Office of the Secretary of State; presentation dated November 13, 2008.

"Missouri—The Cave State," Missouri Department of Natural Resources news release with unknown author, March 2014.

McGuire, John. "It's Geriatric Glitter! In St. Louis An 83-Year Old Reigns as 'Disco Granny,' " *St. Louis Post-Dispatch*, May 23, 1977.

Meyerowitz, Robert. "St. Louis's Brick Thieves," *St. Louis Magazine*, June 8, 2011.

Moore, Doug. "Last Native American Mound in St. Louis is Visited by Tribe that Purchased Site," *St. Louis Post-Dispatch*, March 19, 2013.

Murphy, Doyle. "Take Me to The River," *Riverfront Times*, April 25, 2018.

Naffziger, Chris. "Old Breweries Tell the Forgotten Legacy of Falstaff Beer In St. Louis," *Riverfront Times*, Feb. 4, 2014.

Naffziger, Chris. "Who Were Missouri's German Abolitionists?" *St. Louis Magazine*, March 9, 2016.

O'Neil, Tim. "Gilded Age Hucksterism and Phony Census Boost St. Louis," *St. Louis Post-Dispatch*, July 12, 2014.

O'Neil. Tim. "A Look Back: In 1957 St. Louis Visit, MLK Appeals for End to Racism, Starting in Church Pews," *St. Louis Post-Dispatch*, Dec. 2, 2012.

O'Neil, Tim. "Look Back 250—Steamboats brimming with German and Irish immigrants reshape antebellum St. Louis," *St. Louis Post-Dispatch*, May 31, 2014.

Perez, A.J. "After losing another NFL team, unlikely St. Louis will be able to get another," *USA TODAY* Sports, Jan. 14, 2016.

Petrin, Kae M. "Mid-Century Modern Lustron Homes are Still Standing in St. Louis," *St. Louis Magazine*, July 27, 2017.

Photographic Images, 1904 Louisiana Purchase Exposition--Glass negatives of buildings and displays with various unknown photographers, Missouri History Museum Photograph Archives, Viewed July 31, 2015.

Pistor, Nick. "Pershing or Berlin? A St. Louis Street Name Debate," *St. Louis Post-Dispatch*, Feb. 3, 2014.

Renn, Aaron M. "An Option to the 'Unigov' Example for St. Louis Region." *St. Louis Post-Dispatch*, April 8, 2016.

"Renovated Building Set To Open This Spring." *AAA Midwest Traveler*, May/June 2018.

"Restoration of Old St. Louis Courthouse Fence," *Wrought Rite—Wrought Iron of Distinction, Cast and Wrought Iron*, by Kupferer Bros. Ornamental Iron Works, Inc., Catalog No. 64. Viewed May 25, 2018.

Rushton, Bruce. "Best Underground Railroad Site." *The Riverfront Times*, 2000.

"Saint Louis Zoo Fact Sheet" with unknown author," 8½"×11" sheet, 2016.

"Saint Louis Zoo Wildcare Report" with unknown author," printed booklet, 2014.

Sherman, Susan. "Saint Louis Fashion Fund Announces Eric Johnson as Executive Director of the Saint Louis Fashion Incubator." News release from Saint Louis Fashion Fund. Feb. 17, 2016.

Sorkin, Michael. "Lorraine Dieckmeyer Dies: Sold Town's Best Brain Sandwiches." *St. Louis Post-Dispatch*, March 24, 2011.

Staff and Wire Reports. "Cemeteries Aren't Just For the Dead," *St. Louis Post-Dispatch*, Sept. 25, 2015.

Stiles, Nancy. "10 Things You Didn't Know About Ted Drewes Frozen Custard," *Riverfront Times*, June 18, 2014.

"St. Louis, Missouri City Hall History," City of Saint Louis, printed booklet, 1990.

Taylor, Betsy. "St. Louis fights for a place in Blues history," *USA Today*, Nov. 15, 2009.

"The Shelley House, St. Louis, MO," with unknown author, National Register of Historic Places registration form, April 18, 1988.

"The Shrine of Saint Joseph: Church of Miracles," HDVD. Stepstone Productions, Inc., 2009.

Thomas, Scott. "A Pork Steak Primer," *Feast Magazine*, May 31, 2013.

Toler, Lindsay. "13 Words That Have A Different Meaning In St. Louis," *Riverfront Times*, Jan. 28, 2015.

Toler, Lindsay. "Happy 50th Birthday, St. Louis City Flag!" *Riverfront Times*, Feb. 3, 2014.

Wayman, Norbury L. "History of St. Louis Neighborhoods: Downtown." St. Louis Community Development Center. 1978.

Wayman, Norbury L. "History of St. Louis Neighborhoods: Shaw." St. Louis Community Development Center. 1980.

Weiss, Richard. "The Veiled Prophet Returns To St. Louis For Pomp And Scrutiny," St. Louis Beacon, July 1, 2011.

Wessels, Gloria. "Put More Bite into Zoo-Museum District's Special Audits," *St. Louis Post-Dispatch*, March 29, 2016.


## Websites

"1904 Olympic golf gold medal sells at auction for almost $275,000." Retrieved June 19, 2018. https://thegolfnewsnet.com

"1904 World's Fair-Looking Back at Looking Forward." Retrieved March 3, 2016. http://mohistory.org/FAIR/WF/HTML/Overview/

"A Brief History Of...Beer In St. Louis," Retrieved Aug. 31, 2015. http://www.historyhappenshere.org/node/6866

"A Brief History of the Blues." Retrieved May 4, 2016. http://www.allaboutjazz.com/a-brief-history-of-the-blues-by-ed-kopp.php

"A Preservation Plan for St. Louis, Part I: Historic Contexts, 9--Peopling St. Louis: the Immigration Experience, From the Old Sod." Retrieved January 30, 2018. www.stlouis-mo.gov/government/departments/planning/cultural-resources/preservation-plan/Part-1-Peopling-St-Louis.cfm

"About – Visit The Loop." Retrieved May 6, 2016. http://visittheloop.com/about

"About the ZMD." Retrieved April 7, 2016. http://mzdstl.org/about.html

"Alumni Recall Dr. King's 1964 Visit to SLU." Retrieved June 25, 2018. www.slu.ed./alumni-and-donors/news/mlk-slu-visit.php

"Background on Sgraffito & Art Nouveau." Retrieved June 19, 2018. http://web.nationalbuildingarts.org/recovery-projects/office-buildings/missouri-pacific-buder/

"Ballparks, Arenas and Stadiums: St. Louis Arena-St. Louis, MO." Retrieved May 9, 2016. http://www.ballparks.phanfare.com/2414471

"Basilic of Saint Louis, King, St. Louis, Missouri (The Old Cathedral)." Retrieved Sept. 4, 2015. http://www.oldcathedralstl.org/history.html

"Beer Guide: Saint Louis, Missouri." Retrieved Aug. 31, 2015. http://www.beeradvocate.com/place/city/32/

"Black & White." St. Louis Public Radio. September 4, 2015. www.stlouispublicradio.org/program/black-white

"Blueberry Hill—A landmark St. Louis Restaurant & Music Club." Retrieved May 20, 2016. http://blueberryhill.com/our-story

"Blues History—St. Louis Blues History." Retrieved March 9, 2016. http://blues.nhl.com/club/page.htm?id=39464

"Bocce." Retrieved May 9, 2018. https://www.milosboccegarden.com/bocce/

"Bosnia Memory Project." Retrieved June 18, 2018. https://www.fontbonne.edu/academics/departments/english-and-communication-department/bosnia-memory-project/

"Built St. Louis: Dedicated to the Preservation of Historic Architecture in St. Louis, Missouri." Retrieved Sept. 4, 2015. http://www.builtstlous.net

"Built St. Louis: Vanished Buildings: The Arena." Retrieved May 6, 2016. http://builtstlouis.net/arena01.html

"Built St. Louis: The Watertowers." Retrieved May 6, 2016. http://www.builtstlouis.net/water towers/watertowers1.html

"Catholic Cemeteries of the Archdiocese of St. Louis—Calvary Cemetery." Retrieved Sept. 1, 2015. http://archstl.org/cemeteries/content/view/91/233/

"Charles Lindbergh's Boulevard and the Drive to Rename It," History Happens Here--The Missouri History Museum's blog. March 2, 2010. Retrieved Nov. 9, 2015. http://www.historyhappaneshere.org/archives/1766

"Cherokee Station Business Association-Cherokee Street, St. Louis, Missouri." Retrieved Sept. 4, 2015. http://www.cherokeestation.com/history.html

"Civil Rights Timeline." Retrieved May 11, 2018. http://www.images.mohistory.org/files/civil-rights-timeline.pdf

"City of St. Louis Water Division: Watertowers." Retrieved May 6, 2016. http://www.stlwater.com/watertowers.php

"Climatron Conservatory." Missouri Botanical Garden. Retrieved Sept. 4, 2015. http://www.mobot.org

"Coming in April 2016: Little Black Dress: From Mourning to Night." Missouri History Museum. Retrieved Jan. 15, 2016. http://mohistory.org/node/57334

"Compton Hill Water Tower-City Landmark #13." Retrieved May 6, 2016. https://www.stlouis-mo.gov/government/departments/planning/cultural-resources/city-landmarks/Compton-Hill-Water-Tower.cfm

"Dotage St. Louis: Why Is Everything Brick?" April 14, 2008. Retrieved Sept. 1, 2015. http://stldotage.blogspot.com/2008/04/why-is-everything-brick.html

"Eads Bridge: Construction & Facts." Retrieved May 10, 2018. https://study.com/academy/lesson/eads-bridge-construction-facts.html

"Encyclopedia of Missouri History: Railroads." Retrieved Sept. 1, 2015. http://tacnet.missouri.org/history/encycmo/railroads.html

"Explore St. Louis-Cherokee Street." Retrieved Sept. 4, 2015. http://explorestlouis.com/visit-explore/discover/neighborhoods/cherokee-street/

"Explore St. Louis-Civil War History in St. Louis." Retrieved Sept. 1, 2015. http://explorestlouis.com/visit-explore/discover/itineraries/civil-war-history-in-st-louis/

"Foods of Saint Louis, MO." Retrieved Nov. 5, 2015. http://stlplaces.com/stl_foods/

"Freedom's Gateway-St. Louis In The Civil War." Retrieved Sept. 1, 2015. http://www.freedomsgateway.com/CivilWarinStLouis.aspx

"Garage Sales in St. Louis, Missouri." Retrieved Sept. 4, 2015. http://stlouis. bookoo.com/garage-sales-st.-louis-mo.html?r=10.0

"Gateway Arch Completed." Retrieved May 9, 2016. http://www.history.com/ this-day-in-history/gateway-arch-completed

"Gateway Arch – It's the experience, above all." Retrieved June 20, 2018. www. gatewayarch.com

"German Americans in the War." Retrieved May 10, 2018. http://www. civilwarvirtualmuseum.org/1861-1862/german-americans-in-the-war/ continue-reading.php

"Germans in St. Louis." Retrieved May 10, 2018. https://stlgs.org/research-2/ community/ethnic/germans

"Grant's Farm: Home to History, Wildlife and an Adventure for the Whole Family." Retrieved March 9, 2016. http://www.grantsfarm.com/attractions. html

"History--How This St. Louis Tradition Started." Retrieved Mar. 3, 2016. http://greatforestparkballonrace.com/history

"History-Imo's Pizza." Retrieved Sept. 1, 2015. http://imospizza.com/history/

"History of Barnes-Jewish Hospital." Retrieved May 6, 2016. http://www. barnesjewish.org/About-Us/History

"History of Forest Park." Retrieved March 3, 2016. https://www.stlouis-mo. gov/archive/history-forest-park/early.html

"History of St. Louis Children's Hospital." Retrieved May 6, 2016. http:// www.stlouischildrens.org/about-us/history

"History of St. Louis City Hall." Retrieved June 12, 2018. https://www.stlouis-mo.gov/government/about/history-of-city-hall.cfm

"History of St. Louis Neighborhoods--Marquette-Cherokee." Retrieved Sept. 4, 2015. https://www.stlouis-mo.gov/archive/neighborhood-histories-norbury-wayman/marquette/text17.htm

"History of St. Louis Neighborhoods-The Hill." Retrieved Sept. 1, 2015. https://www.stlouis-mo.gov/archives/neighborhood-histories

"History of the Cathedral Basilica-Cathedral Basilica of St. Louis." Retrieved Sept. 4, 2015. http://cathedralstl.org/parish/parish-history

"Holy Corners." Retrieved May 9, 2018. https://dynamic.stlouis-mo.gov/ history/structdetail.cfm?Master_ID=1359

"Holy Corners-City Landmark #47." Retrieved May 9, 2018. https://www. stlouis-mo.gov/government/departments/planning/cultural-resources/city-landmarks/Holy-Corners.cfm

"Japanese Garden," "Japanese Festival at Missouri Botanical Garden." Retrieved May 11, 2018. http://www.missouribotanicalgarden.org

"KSHE History 1967-1984 – A Brief History of the First 17 Years of The Radio Station." Retrieved May 8, 2018. Kenneth Hawkins, www.youtube.com

"Lindbergh Links: One Road, Two Names; The Difference Is A City Limit." Retrieved Sept. 4, 2015. http://patch.com/missouri/kirkwood/lindbergh-links-one-road-two-names-the-difference-is5c8d5b33a8

"Look Back 250-Gilded Age Hucksterism and Phony Census Boost St. Louis." Retrieved March 8, 2016. http://www.stltoday.com/news/local/metro/look-back

"Louis H. Sullivan Biography." Retrieved March 23, 2016. www.biography.com/people

"Lou Oldani's Restaurant Claimed to be the Birthplace of Toasted Ravioli." *St. Louis Post-Dispatch*. Retrieved Aug. 31, 2015. http://www.stltoday.com/news/local/obituaries/

"Many St. Louis Sites Significant in Black History." Retrieved May 10, 2018. www.explorestlouis.com

"Miracle of St. Peter Claver." Retrieved June 21, 2018. www.shrineofstjoseph.org

"Missouri Botanical Garden – Peonies, Lotus, Azaleas and Rhododendrons, Flowering Cherries." Retrieved May 10, 2018. http://www.missouribotanicalgarden.org

"Missouri Earthquake History." U.S. Geological Survey. Retrieved March 23, 2016. http://www.earthquake.usgs.gov

Missouri History Museum Facebook account post. Retrieved Nov. 17, 2015. http://www.facebook.com/search

"Missouri Pacific Building (Buder Building)." Retrieved June 19, 2018. http://web.nationalbuildingarts.org/recovery-projects/office-buildings/missouri-pacific-buder/

"Missouri—The Cave State." Missouri Caves Association. Retrieved Apr. 12, 2016. http://missouricaves.com/caves/

"Moonrise Hotel-Joe Edwards." Retrieved May 6, 2016. http://moonrisehotel.com/joe-edwards/

"Mound City on the Mississippi, a St. Louis History." St. Louis Historic Preservation. Retrieved Apr. 19, 2016. http://stlcin.missouri.org/history/structdetail.cfm?Master_ID=2090

"National Blues Museum strengthens St. Louis' bond with genre." Retrieved May 4, 2016. https://www/national_bluesmuseum.org/news/

"Neighborhoods." Retrieved Feb. 15, 2016. http://explorestlouis.com/visit-explore/discover/neighborhoods/

"Old Courthouse." Retrieved May 6, 2016. https://www.nps.gov/jeff/planyourvisit/och.htm

"Open For Business Year-Round!-Ballpark Village." Retrieved Feb. 17, 2016. http://stlouis.cardinals.mlb.com/stl/ballpark/information/index

"Our Beers—Urban Chestnut Brewing Company. Retrieved Jan. 19, 2016. http://urbanchestnut.com/our-beers/

"Physical Growth of the City of Saint Louis." St. Louis City Plan Commission-1969. Retrieved Sept. 4, 2015. https://www.stlouis-mo.gov/archive/ihistory-physical-growth-stlouis/

Pohlmann, Mark. "Stop Sign Warrants," ITE District 4 Journal. Retrieved Apr. 12, 2016. http://www.midwesternite.org/FallJournal/StopSignWarrants.htm

"Portraits in the Graveyard: An Unexpected Look Into the History of Organized Crime in St. Louis." Retrieved March 23, 2016. https://astumblingcontradiction.wordpress.com

"Provelology: The Study of a Made-Up Cheese With a Made-Up Name." Retrieved Dec. 3, 2015. http://www.stltoday.com/lifestyles/food-and-cooking/

"Readers: St. Louis Has Too Many Stop Signs." *Urban Review*, Saint Louis. Retrieved Apr. 11, 2016. http://www.urbanreviewstl.com/2014/03/readers-st-louis-has-too-many-stop-signs/

"Remembering Early KSHE Radio." Retrieved May 8, 2018. On StL Videos, www.youtube.com

"Rigazzi's-St. Louis Restaurant on The Hill." Retrieved Jan. 26, 2018. www.rigazzis.com

"River des Peres Watershed Coalition." Retrieved Feb. 15, 2016. http:riverdesperes.org/explore/timeline

"Something in the Water: A Saint Louis Rockumentary." Retrieved May 8, 2018. HECTV St. Louis, www.youtube.com

"Soulard Farmers Market St. Louis." Retrieved Sept. 4, 2015. http://soulardmarketstl.com/about-soulard-market/

"Spirits of St. Louis." Retrieved May 6, 2016. https://enwikipedia.org/wiki/Spirits_of_St._Louis

"St. Louis Beer Guide." Retrieved Aug. 31, 2015. http://stlhops.com/st-lous-beer-guide

"Saint Louis Downtown Map." Saint Louis Front Page. Retrieved April 8, 2016. http://www.slfp.com/CityScapes.html

St. Louis Cardinals (1960-1987)." Retrieved May 10, 2016. http://wwwsportsencyclopedia.com/nfl/azstl/cardinals.html

"St. Louis City Revised Code Chapter 15.156: Division IX. Miscellaneous Offenses and Regulations: Yard Sales." Retrieved Sept. 4, 2015. http://www.slpl.lib.mo.us/cco/code/data/t15156.htm

"St. Louis Hawks (1955-1968)." http://www.sportsencyclopedia.com/nba/stlhawks.html

"St. Louis, Missouri, Code of Ordinances, ordinance 17.02.500 – Stop." Retrieved Apr. 12, 2016.https://www.municode.com/library/mo/st._louis/codes/code_of_ordinances?nodeld=TIT17VETR_DIVITRCO_CH17.02DE_17.02.010GE

"St. Louis Union Station." Retrieved Sept. 1, 2015. http://www.stlouisunionstations.com/about

"St. Patrick's Day Parade." Retrieved Mar. 3, 2016. https://irishparade.org/the-parade/

"Terminal Railroad Association of St. Louis-TRRA History." Retrieved Nov. 9, 2015. http://www.terminalrailroad.com

"'Test Elephant' Proves Eads Bridge is Safe; 14 June, 1874." Retrieved May 11, 2018. https://www.historychannel.com/au/articles

"The Germans Save St. Louis for the Union," by Patrick Young, Esq. Retrieved May 10, 2018. www.longislandwins.com

"The Great Forest Park Balloon Race." Retrieved Mar. 3, 2016. http:stlouis.about.com

"The Great Ice Cream/Frozen Custard Debate," Retrieved Nov. 9, 2015. http://www.chefs.edu/student-life/culinary-central/april-2012/the-great-ice-cream-frozen-custard-debate

"The History of Frozen Custard." Retrieved Sept. 4, 2015. http://www.rebco2000.com/ollies

"The History Of IBC Root Beer," Retrieved Feb. 4, 2016. http://www.ibcrootbeer.com/history.aspx

"The History of Italy's Second Favorite Sport – Bocce Ball." Retrieved January 26, 2018. http://ciaostl.com

"The History of St. Louis Municipal Bath House," nextSTL, May 6, 2016. https://nextstl.com/2012/12/the-history-of-the-st-louis-municipal-bath-house/

"The Last Standing Mound in Mound St. Louis City Is For Sale." Retrieved Feb. 26, 2016. www.landmarks-stl.org/news

"The Many Mysteries of 'Our' Mostaccioli." St. Louis Post-Dispatch. Retrieved Aug. 31. 2015. https://www.questia.com/newspaper/

"The Mystery of St. Louis's Veiled Prophet." Retrieved Jan. 19, 2016. http://www.theatlantic.com/politics/archive/2014/09

"The Official Site of the St. Louis Cardinals." Retrieved March 23, 2016. http://stlouis.cardinals.mlb.com

"The Residences at Holy Corners." Retrieved May 11, 2018. http://liveholycorners.com

"The Rising Fourth City (1890-1904)." St. Louis Turns 250 in 2014. Retrieved Sept. 1, 2015. http://www.stl250.org/crash-course-fourth-city.aspx

"The State & Indian Streets of South St. Louis." Distilled History. Retrieved Apr. 9, 2016. http://www.distilledhistory.com/streets/

"The Summer of Eads," Parts 1, 3, 4. Distilled History. Retrieved May 11, 2018. http://www.distilledhistory.com

"Toasted Ravioli, The Secret of St. Louis." *New York Times*. Retrieved Aug. 31, 2015. http://www.nytimes.com/1987/02/25/

"True Champion: Mind & Body Sports Training." Retrieved May 18, 2018.

"Twenty-five Mafia Cities." Retrieved September 1, 2015. http://americanmafia.com

"Twisted History." Retrieved Aug. 31, 2015. http://guspretzels.com

"U.S. Army Corps of Engineers--Eagle Watching." Retrieved Nov. 9, 2015. http://www/mvs.usace.army.mi/missions/recreation/eaglewatching.aspx

"U.S. Army Corps of Engineers—St. Louis District." Retrieved May 11, 2018. http://www.mvs.usace.army.mil

"Veiled Prophet Organization-History." Retrieved Jan. 12, 2016. http://www.veiledprophet.org/history

"Visitors Guide to the Middle Mississippi River Valley." Retrieved Nov. 9, 2015. http://www.greatriverroad.com

"Visitors Guide to the Old Courthouse National Historic Site." Retrieved June 12, 2018. http://greatriverroad.com/stlouis/oldcourt.htm

"Welcome to City Museum, Where Imagination Runs Wild!" Retrieved April 7, 2016. http://www.citymuseum.org/pages/about-us-creative/

"Welcome to the Italia-America Bocce Club." Retrieved May 9, 2018. https://www.stlbocce.com

"Welcome to the Old Courthouse!" Retrieved June 12, 2018. https://www.nps.gov/jeff/planyourvisit/och.htm

## Interviews & E-Mails

Anonymous Source, U.S. National Park Service ranger; interview with author June 12, 2018.

Anonymous Source, St. Louis Blues Hockey Club; interview with author March 22, 2016.

Behle, Pat, Columbia Bottom Conservation Area-Missouri Department of Conversation; interview with author Feb. 3, 2016.

Bolin, Norma M., lawyer; interview with author April 1, 2016.

Burkett, Sue, librarian, Kirkwood Historical Society; interview with author Feb. 26, 2016.

Carlson, Mike, son of co-owner, Schottzie's Bar and Grill; interview with author Jan. 22, 2016.

Carney, Jon, meteorologist, National Weather Service; e-mail to author Feb. 18, 2016.

Clanton, Terry, owner, World's Fair Donuts; interview with author Feb. 26, 2016.

Colligan, Andrew, archivist, Missouri Botanical Garden; interview with author Feb. 16, 2016, June 8, 2018.

Cooksey, Talan, Park Avenue Coffee; interview with author Feb. 16, 2016.

DeWitt, Matt, counselor, Calvary Cemetery; interview with Jan. 13, 2016.

Erwin, Jim, writer & Civil War historian; e-mail to author Feb. 18, 2016.

Gallagher, Susan, director of public relations, Saint Louis Zoo; interview with author March 9, 2016.

Goldfeder, Mark, St. Louis streetcar enthusiast; interview with author May 21, 2018.

Grant's Farm Tour Representative; interview with author June 18, 2018.

Guinan, Patrick E., extension/state climatologist, University of Missouri; e-mail to author March 16, 2016.

Harmon, Dale, former St. Louis University soccer team member; interview with author May 25, 2018.

Heerlein, Nicole, spokesperson, Cathedral Basilica of Saint Louis; interview with author Jan. 19, 2016.

Holleman, Joe, *St. Louis Post-Dispatch*; interview with author Feb. 16, 2016.

Jones, Gabe, spokesperson, Archdiocese of St. Louis; interviews with author Jan. 15, 2016; Jan. 18, 2016; June 21, 2018.

Keeven-Franke, Dorris, executive director, Missouri Germans Consortium; interview with author June 16, 2018.

Kelly, Bill, senior educator, James. S. McDonnell Planetarium at the Saint Louis Science Center; interview with author Feb. 18, 2016.

Koebbe, Gus III, Gus' Pretzels; interview with author Jan. 13, 2016.

Kuplent, Florian, brewmeister, Urban Chestnut; interview with author Jan. 28, 2016.

Lang, Charlotte, St. Peter Catholic Church, St. Charles; interview with author June 14, 2018.

Lay, Richard, vice president, Bellefontaine Cemetery Association; interview with author Jan. 13, 2016.

Lowery, Robert Sr., member of St. Louis' Major Case Squad, the St. Louis Strike Force on Organized Crime, and a former Florissant mayor; interview with author April 6, 2016.

Merkel, Jim, writer; interview with author Feb. 4, 2016.

Meyer, Shannon, senior curator, Missouri History Museum; interview with author July 31, 2015.

Michler, Terry, soccer coach, Christian Brothers College High School; interview with author May 18, 2018.

Rhomberg, Greg R., owner, Antique Warehouse; e-mails to author Feb. 3, 2016, Feb. 4, 2016.

Rosen, Rick, Landmarks Association of St. Louis, volunteer coordinator; e-mails to author Feb. 15, 2016.

Rugg, Marji, owner's daughter, Courtesy Diner/Hampton Ave.; interview with author Jan. 22, 2016.

Runde, Stephen J., Director of Streets, City of St. Louis, interview with author Apr. 14, 2016.

Savio, Tom, owner, Milo's Tavern and Bocce Garden on The Hill, interview with author June 11, 2018.

Sherman, Susan, Saint Louis Fashion Incubator; interview with author Feb. 17, 2016.

Spencer, Dr. Thomas M., author and director of honors student affairs, Eastern Illinois University; e-mails with author Feb. 15, 2016 and March 7, 2016.

Stevens, Ron, producer, broadcast veteran, and former KSHE 95 disc jockey: interview with author May 11, 2018.

Storm, Max, founder, 1904 World's Fair Society, Inc.; interview with author Jan. 15, 2016.

Torbert, Dr. Benjamin, University of Missouri-St. Louis; e-mails to author March 9, 2016.

Vines, Randy, STL-Style; e-mail with author May 16, 2018.

Vogt, Samantha, owner's assistant, Charlie Gitto's; interview with author Jan. 22, 2016.

Weil, Andrew, director, Landmarks Association of St. Louis; e-mails with author Feb. 16, 2016.

Zimmerman, Ronald N., American Society of Civil Engineers and St. Louis Museum of Transportation volunteer; e-mails with author Feb. 24, 2016.

# PHOTO CREDITS

Images not listed below are believed to be in the public domain.

Antiques Warehouse 16 (top left), 128 (left)

Bidgee via Wikipedia Commons 171

David Baugher, 50

Don Korte 3, 8 (top), 10 (right), 13, 15, 17 (top), 19 (both), 21, 31, 33, 41 (bottom right), 56 (inset), 56 (top right), 58 (street signs), 59 (top), 62, 64, 65, 67 (both), 75 (both), 76, 78, 80 (both), 81 (top left), 82, 100 (both), 110 (background), 111 (top right), 116 (right), 119 (top left), 123 (bottom), 129, 135, 136 (background), 139, 142, 174, 177, 178, 185, 186 (top right)

Library of Congress 6, 10 (top left), 12, 18 (right), 20 (bottom right), 32, 34, 35, 37, 41 (top left), 44 (bottom right), 48, 53, 54, 60 (top right), 68, 70, 104, 106, 107 (bottom left), 110 (bottom right), 112, 113 (top right), 115, 116 (bottom right), 119 (top left), 123 (top right), 126 (inset), 129, 134, 136 (inset), 138 (right), 140, 141, 154, 156, 168 (bottom), 172, 176, 187 (bottom right)

Jim Merkel 11, 93

iStock, 24

Missouri Digital Heritage 115 (bottom right)

Missouri History Museum 14, 17 (bottom left), 27 (top right, bottom right), 29, 46, 30, 36, 38, 39, 42, 43, 51, 56, 60 (background, bottom right), 63, 72, 73 (top right), 74, 81 (bottom left, right), 101, 103, 107 (bottom right), 108, 109 (top right), 111, 112 (inset), 114, 120, 124, 125, 126 (bottom), 128 (top), 138 (left), 143, 144, 146, 147, 149, 150, 158, 161, 163, 165, 168 (top), 169, 170, 172, 175 (top right), 182, 184

Nheyob via Wikipedia Commons 132

Paul Sableman via Wikipedia Commons 166

Pixabay 23, 58, 152

St. Louis Mercantile Library 187 (top left)

Valerie Battle Kienzle 84–92, 94–99, 130

Reedy Press 40

Shutterstock 44, 162

# INDEX

1904 Summer Olympics, 176, 177
1904 World's Fair, 7, 31, 49, 80, 122, 130, 136, 174, 176, 177
1904 World's Fair Society, 174, 176
7UP, 40, 41
ABC Bohemian, 38
Abolitionists, 117
Aeronautics, 170
Air traffic controller, 171
American Basketball Association, 149
American League, 130, 148
Andy's frozen custard, 125
Anti-German sentiment, 67
Antique Warehouse, 40
Arboretum, 141
Archdiocese of St. Louis, 22, 23, 112, 134, 140, 153, 179, 183
Arctic, 28, 33
Art Hill, 175
BJC Health Systems, 129
Bald eagles, 32
Balloon glow, 173
Balloon race, 173
Balloonists, 170, 172, 173
Ballpark Village, 144, 145
Baden, 51, 67
Barkus Pet Parade, 186
Barnes Hospital, 129
Barnett, Haynes and Barnett, 185
Basilica of Saint Louis, King of France, the Parish of St. Louis (Old Cathedral), 22, 108, 179, 182, 183
Bass, Fontella, 105
Bath houses, 167
Beaver, 23
Beer, 2, 7, 23, 38, 39, 40, 41, 43, 57, 69, 75, 139, 141, 181
Behle, Pat, 32
Bellefontaine Cemetery, 130, 141
Belvederes, 113
Bends, the, 111
Benoist, Thomas, 171

Benton Park, 51
Berry, Albert, 171
Bevo Mill, 51, 169
Bissell "New Red" water tower, 35
Boyle Avenue, 55
Black Lives Matter Movement, 115
Blodwyn Pig, 132
Blow, Susan, 141
Blueberry Hill Restaurant, 69
Blues music, 104, 105, 130
Bocce, 154, 155
Boeing Company, The, 171
Bolin, Norma M., 55
Bosnia Memory Project, 169
Bosnians, 168, 169
Brain sandwich, 8, 9
Brentwood, 51
Breweries, 38, 39, 130, 181, 187
Bricks, 122, 160
Brock, Lou, 145
Bronze medal, 177
Brookings Hall, 174
Brown, A.D., 131
Brown, George Warren, 131
Brown Shoe Company, 131, 188
Budweiser Beer, 38, 139
Budweiser Clydesdales, 139
Burek, 6, 7
Burkett, Sue, 62
Busch, Adolphus, 138, 141
Busch, August A. "Gussie" Jr., 138, 139
Busch Stadium, 144, 145, 149
Buster Brown Shoes, 131
Caleres, 131
Calvary Cemetery, 140, 141
Cardiac Cardinals, 149
Cardinals Nation, 144
Carlson, Bob, 9
Carlson, Mike, 9
Carney, Jon, 25, 27, 28, 29
Carondelet, 51

Carroll Street, 74
Cars, 55
Cassilly, Bob, 78
Cathedral Basilica of Saint Louis
  (New Cathedral), 182, 183
Catholic Church, 22, 23, 112, 134,
  178, 179, 182, 183
Catholic Youth Council, 153
Cave Resources Act, 39
Caves, 38, 39, 79
Cave State, The, 39
Census, 49
Central West End, 51, 181
Cerveza, 6, 7
Charles, Ray, 104
Charlie Gitto's Restaurant, 11
Checkerdome, The, 151
Cherokee Street, 56, 57
Chicago, Illinois, 43, 47, 49, 54, 61, 63,
  133, 171, 176, 177
Chopin, Kate, 141
Chouteau, August, 122, 179
Chateau de Chambord, 113
Cheltenham syncline, 159
Children's Zoo, 83
Chippewa Street, 63, 124, 125
Chouteau Avenue, 59
Chouteau Park, 137
Christ Church Cathedral, 115
Christian Brothers College High
  School, 152
Christian Health Services, 129
Civil Courts Building, 109, 165
City Museum, 78, 79
Cities of the Dead, 140
City Museum, 78, 79
Civil Courts Building, 109, 165
Civil War, 6, 49, 104, 108, 116, 141,
  152
Clanton, Terry, 18
Clark, William, 141
Claver, Peter, 135
Clay, 159, 160
Climatron, 102, 103
Clothing industry, 188
Coldwater Creek, 37
Colligan, Andrew, 103, 142, 143
Columbia Bottom Conservation Area,
  32

Compton Hill water tower, 35
Confederacy, 117
Cooksey, Talan, 21
Courtesy Diner, 17
Crestwood, 51, 109, 133
Crown Candy Kitchen, 167
Curtiss, Glenn, 170
Curtiss-Robertson Company, 171
Curtiss-Wright Company, 171
Davis, Miles, 105
Dean, Dizzy, 145
Delmar Boulevard, 68
Delmar Loop (The Loop), 41, 68, 69,
  181
Denny Road, 62, 63
DeWitt, Matt, 141
Donuts, 18, 19, 75
Drewes, Ted, 124, 125
Drewes, Ted Sr., 124
Dulles International Airport, 107
Eads Bridge, 49, 60, 110, 111
Eads, James Buchanan, 110
Earthquakes, 26, 27, 107
Eastern Illinois University, 127
Edison Brothers, 188
Edwards, Joe, 68, 69, 73
Edwards, Linda, 68
Emancipation proclamation, 117
Engelmann, George, 143
Enterprise Center, 147, 151
Fabulous Fox Theater, 181
Fair Saint Louis, 186, 187
Fairgrounds Park, 80
Falstaff Beer, 38
Father of Modern American
  Architecture, 165
Federko, Bernie, 150
Filling station, 55
First Church of Christ, Scientist, 184
Fish-bowl beer, 7
Fish fries, 22, 23
Fitz's Bottling Company, 41
Fitz's Root Beer, 41
Fitz's soft drinks, 41
Fleur de Lis, 110, 165
Flight Cage, 80, 175
Florissant, Missouri, 43
Food, 2, 4, 5, 6, 7, 8, 9, 10, 12, 14, 16,
  17, 19, 20, 21, 22, 33, 69, 152, 154,
  160, 161, 168, 181

Food Network, 21
Forest Park, 69, 73, 77, 80, 81, 123, 136, 137, 170, 172, 173, 174, 175, 184
Forest Park's Central Field, 172
Four-family flats, 162
Fourth City, The, 48
Fox-Wohl shoes, 188
French Renaissance Revival, 113
Friedman-Shelby shoes, 188
Fritz's frozen custard, 125
Frog legs, 23
Frozen custard, 124, 125
Fuller, Buckminster, 102
Garage sales, 120, 121
Garment district, 188, 189
Gasbags, 173
Gast beer, 34
Gateway Arch, 32, 64, 106, 108, 182, 187
Gateway Arch National Park, 106, 187
*Gemini*/McDonnell-Douglas, 83, 171
German American, 67
Germans, 116, 117
Ghost signs, 70
Gibson, Bob, 145
Goldfeder, Mark, 72
Gooey butter cake, 11, 20, 21
Grafman, Shelley, 133
Grand Avenue, 35, 55, 181
Grand "Old White" water tower, 35
Grand Oracle, 126
Grant, Ulysses S., 138
Grant's Farm, 138, 139
Grantwood Village, 51
Gravois Park, 137
Gravois Road, 51, 138
Grbic, 7
Great Forest Park Balloon Race, 172
Great Plains, 25, 28
Griesedieck, 38
Grigg, C. L., 41
Grove, The, 181
Groves, Albert B., 185
Guinan, Pat, 29
Gulf of Mexico, 25, 28
Gus' Pretzels, 2
Handy, W. C., 104
Heerlein, Nicole, 183

Hill, The, 51, 154, 155, 160, 161
Hitch team, 139
Hoffman, Alan, 170
Holleman, Joe, 47, 119, 120, 187
Holy Corners, 184, 185
Home brews, 40
Hoosier, 44, 45
Horgan, Bob, 153
Hot-air balloons, 172, 173
Hotel de Ville, 113
Howdy Orange, 40
Humidity, 24, 25
Hyde, Dr. Brett, 47
Hyde Park beer, 38
IBC Root Beer, 40
Illinois River, 32, 60, 122
Immigrants, 3, 6, 11, 38, 47, 113, 116, 117, 152, 154, 157, 160, 163
Imo's, 5
Independence Day, 127
Italia-America Bocce Club, 155
International Air Tournament, 170
International Shoe Company, 188
Jackson, Claiborne, 117
James S. McDonnell Planetarium, 82
Japanese American Citizens League (JACL), 142
Japanese Festival, 143, 186
Japanese Garden (Seiwa-en), 142
Jefferson Bank, 115
Jefferson Barracks, 171
Jefferson National Expansion Memorial, 187
Jefferson, Thomas, 107
Jewel Box, 175
Jewish Hospital, 129
Johnson, Lonnie, 105
Jones, Gabe, 22, 23, 112, 153, 179, 183
*Joy of Cooking, The*, 16
Junior-size clothing, 189
KSHE 95, 132, 133
Karagiannis, Harry, 7
Kasseri cheese, 7
Kawana, Koichi, 142
Keeven-Franke, Dorris, 117
Kelly, Bill, 83
Kiel Auditorium, 115, 148
Kiel Center, 151
King Louis IX, 179
King Mausolus, 165

King, The Rev. Dr. Martin Luther, Jr., 115
Kingdom of Khorassan, 126
Kinloch Field, 171
Kirkwood Historical Society, 62
Kirkwood, James P., 62
Kirkwood, Missouri, 19, 62, 63, 72
Kirkwood Road, 62, 63
Koebbe, Gus III, 2
Krekel, Arnold, 117
Kupferer Bros. Ornamental Iron Works, Inc., 109
Kuplent, Florian, 181
Laclede Gas Light Company, 173
Laclede, Pierre, 59, 64, 122, 179
Lafayette Park, 137
Lafayette Square, 21
Lambert, Albert Bond, 170
Lambert-St. Louis Flying Field, 171
Lambert-St. Louis Municipal Airport, 171
Landmarks Association of St. Louis, 159, 160, 162, 164
Lay, Richard, 141
League, Archie, 171
Lemp Brewery, 38
Lent, 22, 23
Lincoln University, 117
Lindbergh Boulevard, 62, 63
Lindbergh, Charles, 171, 185
Lindell Boulevard, 55
Link, Theodore C., 184
Linnaeus, Carl, 143
Living World, 83
Loop, The, 68, 69, 181
Loop Trolley Transportation District, 69
LouFest Music Festival, 186
Louie, 147
Louisiana Purchase, 107, 174
Louisiana Purchase Exposition (1904 World's Fair), 31, 49, 174
Lowery, Robert Sr., 43
Mad cow disease, 9
Mafia, 43
Mann, George Richard, 113
Maplewood, 19, 51
March on Washington for Jobs and Freedom, 115
Mardi Gras, 186

Market Street, 65
Maull's Barbeque Sauce, 13
Mauran, Russell and Garden, 185
McCullough, Anne, 57
McDonnell Aircraft, 83, 171
McDonnell-Douglas, 171
Meat substitutes, 23
Meachum, Mary, 114
Meramec Caverns, 39
*Mercury*/McDonnell-Douglas, 83, 171
Meskerem, 7
Meteorology, 29
MetroLink, 111
Metropolitan Zoological Park and Museum District, 76, 208
Meyer, Shannon, 189
Michler, Terry, 152
Microfest, 39
Migratory birds, 32
Military aviation, 171
Milo's Tavern and Bocce Garden, 154
Milwaukee Athletic Club, 177
Minnesota and Hill Park, 137
Miracles, 134
Mississippi, 105
Mississippi flyway, 32
Mississippi River, 26, 29, 32, 36, 37, 49, 51, 59, 60, 62, 104, 107, 110, 111, 114, 119, 122, 123, 129, 159, 162, 179
Mississippi Valley, 25
Missouri Botanical Garden, 18, 76, 77, 102, 103, 142, 143, 186
Missouri Botanical Garden's Japanese Festival, 143, 186
Missouri Department of Conservation, 32
Missouri Department of Natural Resources, 39
Missouri Germans Consortium, 117
Missouri History Museum, 73, 76, 137, 175, 189
Missouri River, 29, 32, 60, 119, 122, 162
MonstroCity, 79
Moonrise Hotel, 69
Moonshine, 40
Moore, Alice, 105
Mosaics, 79, 182, 183
Mostaccioli, 14, 15

Mother Road, The, 54, 55, 125
Mound City, 122, 123
Mounds, 122, 123
Mount Pleasant Park, 137
Mr. Wizard's, 125
Mud House, The, 17
Muench, Friedrich, 117
Municipal Bathhouses, 166
Municipal Opera (The Muny), 137, 175
Municipalities, 50, 51
Musial, Stan, 111, 145
Nagano, Japan, 143
National Guard, 171
National Basketball Association, 149
National Blues Museum, 104, 105
National Collegiate Athletic Association, 153
National Dairy Show, 150
National Historic Civil Engineering Landmark, 111
National Historic Landmark, 61, 111
National Hockey League, 147
National League, 144, 145, 148
National League Pennant, 145
National Register Historic District, 185
National Register of Historic Places, 35, 123, 135, 163, 165
National Underground Railroad Network to Freedom, 109
National Weather Service, 25
Natural refrigeration, 38
Naturalizer shoes, 131
Never Say Goodbye: The KSHE Documentary, 133
New Madrid, Missouri, 26, 27
Note, The, 147
Notre Dame Cathedral, 135
OSHA regulations, 71
Obata, Gyo, 83
Octoberfest, 186
O'Fallon, Missouri, 51
Old Courthouse, 108, 109, 114, 187,
Olive Street, 51, 65, 163
Olive Street Terra Cotta District, 163
Olympic Committee, 176
Onondaga Cave, 39
Orange Smile, 40
Organized crime, 42, 43

Osage Nation, 123
Ozark Plateau, 25
Pacific Railroad, 62
Pageant, The, 69, 126
Pallino, 154
Parabola, 106
Park Avenue Coffee, 21
Party Town, 186
Peabody Opera House, 181
Peacock Loop Diner, 69
Penrose, 51
Pershing, General John, 67
Philadelphia, Pennsylvania, 59, 66
Pho Grand, 7
Pin-Up Bowl, 69
Plager, Barclay, 150
Plante, Jacques, 150
Plexiglas, 103
Pneumatic caissons, 110
Poage, George Coleman, 177
Pork steaks, 12, 13
Powell Symphony Hall, 181
Power Play, 147
Pretzels, 2, 3
Privy vault, 167
Prohibition, 40, 139
Pronunciations, 46, 47, 113
Provel, 4, 5
Public Bath Houses, 166, 167
Public Bath Movement, 166
Queen of Love and Beauty, 127
Quigley, James, 109
Racquet Club, 185
Railroads, 36, 60, 61, 130, 162
Ralston Purina, 151
Ranoush, 7
Reavis, Logan Uriah, 49
Redbird Fever, 144
Red Goose shoes, 131
Rickey, Branch, 145
Rigazzi's, 7
River des Peres (River of the Fathers), 30, 31
Roberts, Johnson & Rand, 188
Rhomberg, Greg R., 40
Rolling stop, 52, 53
Rombauer, Irma, 16
Roosevelt, President Franklin D., 139
Roosevelt, President Theodore, 170
Rosen, Rick, 162, 164

Route 66, 54, 55, 63, 125
Rugg, Larry, 17
Rugg, Marji, 17
Rural Cemetery Movement, 140
SSM Health, 129
Saarinen, Eero, 107
Saganaki, 7
St. Louis, Missouri 6, 35, 51, 55, 59, 77, 80, 83, 107, 108, 109, 136, 137, 179
Saint Louis Art Museum, 76, 175
Saint Louis Brewery, 39
Saint Louis Fashion Fund, 189
Saint Louis Science Center, 76, 82, 83
Saint Louis University, 114, 115, 129, 153
Saint Louis Zoo, 76, 80, 82, 81, 83, 136, 175
Salomon, Sid, 150
Santa Monica, California, 54
Savio, Tom, 154
Schlafly products, 39
Schorr-Kolkschneider beer, 38
Schottzie's Bar and Grill, 9
Schweiger's Produce, 75
Scott, Dred and Harriet, 108, 114, 141
Scovill, Paul, 153
Seattle, Washington, 55
Second Baptist Church, 185
Seven Wonders of the Ancient World, 165
Sgrafitto/sgraffiti, 163
Shaw, Henry, 66, 143
Shelley, J. D. and Ethel, 115
Sherman, William Tecumseh, 141
Shoe City, U.S.A., 131
Shoe industry, 130
Shoes, 130, 131
Show-Me State, 63
Shrine of St. Joseph, 134, 135
Shrine of St. Joseph Friends, 135
Skillman, Dan, 137
Slinger, 16, 17
Smith, Ozzie, 145
Smithsonian Institute, 80, 175
Snowy Owls, 33
Soccer, 152, 153
Soft drinks, 40, 41
Soulard Farmers Market, 19, 74, 75
Soulard, Julia, 74

South Grand Avenue, 181
South St. Louis, 9, 11, 30, 57, 159, 160, 169, 172
Spencer, Dr. Thomas M., 127
*Spirit of St. Louis, The*, 171, 185
Spirits of St. Louis, 148, 149
Spiro's Greek Restaurant, 7
Sportsman's Park, 149
St. John's Methodist Church, 184
St. Joseph Catholic Church, 134, 135
St. Louis Arena (The Barn), 149, 150, 151
St. Louis Astronomical Society, 83
St. Louis Blues Hockey Club, 146, 147, 150, 151
"St. Louis Blues" (song), 104
St. Louis Browns, 130, 148
St. Louis Cardinals, 32, 144, 145, 148
St. Louis Cardinals (football), 149
St. Louis Children's Hospital, 129
St. Louis City Hall, 113
St. Louis City Revised Code, 121
St. Louis Community Development Agency, 66
St. Louis County, 37, 51, 77, 108, 119, 156, 157
St. Louis Department of Streets, 52
St. Louis Garment District, 188, 189
St. Louis Hawks, 148
St. Louis Major Case Squad, 43
St. Louis, Missouri, Code of Ordinances, 53
St. Louis Museum of Transportation, 60
*St. Louis Post-Dispatch*, 47, 73, 119, 120, 187
St. Louis Rams, 148, 149
St. Louis Strike Force On Organized Crime, 43
St. Louis Walk of Fame, 69
St. Nicholas Greek Festival, 186
St. Patrick's Day parades, 186
St. Paul sandwich, 7
St. Peter Catholic Church, St. Charles, 23
Stan Musial Veterans Memorial Bridge, 111
Standpipes, 34, 35
Stanley Cup, 147
Statue of Liberty, 107

State climatologist, 29
Stephen and Peter Sachs Museum Building, 143
Stevens, Ron, 133
Strecker, Ignatius, 134
Streetcar track, 72
Streetcars, 57, 65, 69, 72, 73
Steinberg Memorial Skating Rink, 175
Stop signs, 52, 53
Storm, Max, 174, 176
Strychnine, 177
Sugarloaf Mound, 123
Sullivan, Louis H., 164
Sumner High School
Super Bowl XXXIV, 114
Sweetmeat, 132, 133
Sydney, Australia, 107
Sydney Opera House, 107
Taft, William Howard, 131
Taylor, Eva, 105
Taylor Park, 137
Teahouse, 143
Teasdale, Sara, 141
Temple Israel, 83, 115
Terminal Railroad Association of St. Louis (TRRA), 60
Terra cotta, 35, 163
Tivoli Theater, 69
Toasted ravioli (T-ravs), 10, 11
*Today* show, 21
Torbert, Dr. Benjamin, 47
Tower Grove East, 51
Tower Grove Park, 137
Townsend, Henry, 105
Travel Channel, 11
Tucker Boulevard, 165
Tulip chair, 107
TUMS antacid, 17
Tuscan Masonic Temple, 185
U. City Loop, 73
UNcola, The, 41
Underground Railroad, 109, 114, 116
Unger, Garry, 150
Union Army, 116, 117
Union Station, 61, 83, 184
United Hebrew Temple, 115
University City, 51, 68, 69, 73, 171, 181
University of Missouri-St. Louis, 47

Urban Chestnut Brewing Company, 39, 181
Utzon, Jorn, 107
U.S. Army Corps of Engineers, 36, 37
U.S. Bocce Championship, 155
U.S. National Park Service's National Underground Railroad Network to Freedom, 109
U.S. Patent and Trademark Office, 5
U.S. Supreme Court, 108, 115
Veiled Prophet, 126, 127
Vernacular, 47, 113
VESS, 40
VESS soda bottle, 40
Vocabulary, 44, 47
Vogt, Samantha, 11
Wainwright Building, 164, 165
Wainwright, Ellis, 165
Walldogs, 71
Warm Springs Ranch, 139
Washington Avenue, 131, 181, 188, 189
Washington Tabernacle Baptist Church, 115
Washington University, 47, 83, 129, 174, 177
Watershed, 33
Watson Road, 55, 63
Wayman, Norbury L., 66
Weather, 24, 25, 26, 28, 29
Weil, Andrew, 159, 160, 162
Wellston Loop, 72
Weninger, Francis Zavier, 135
Whistle, 40
Wine, 23
World Series Championship, 145, 148
World's Fair Donuts, 18
Williams, Tennessee, 141
Wright Brothers, 170
Yard toilet, 167
Zamboni machines, 147
Zia's on the Hill, 15
Zimmer, Ronald N., 60, 61
Zimmern, Andrew, 9
Zoo-Museum District, 77
Zoological Board of Control, 81
Zoological Society of St. Louis, 81